Easy 'n Healthy Cooking

Diana Fong Chan

Have fun cooking

Diana F. Chan

About the Author

Diana Chan is a creative innovator with a passion for cooking and baking. She was born in Shanghai, China and grew up in Hong Kong and Brazil where she watched her family's Chinese chef prepare simple daily meals and elaborate banquet dishes. Watching the chef was a natural way for her to learn the basics of Chinese cooking which facilitated her transition into Fusion cooking later. Diana has a knack for analyzing favorite dishes, replicating them, or creating innovative variations of her own and enjoys having family and friends over to sample her new creations. She and her husband are docent trainees at the Asian Art Museum in San Francisco. She loves art, music and dance and plays the piano to relax and to get inspirational ideas for cooking. She did most of the photography and all the illustrations for the book which began as a small collection of recipes for family and mushroomed into a full scale cookbook.

With Martin Yan at The Asian
Gourmet celebration

With Chef Chu at El Camino Hospital
Fundraiser Banquet at Chef Chu's

Buying yam leaves at the farmer's market

China Tour with Professor Riegel and
Docent Trainees, Asian Art Museum, S.F.

Editor
Susan Fong

Graphic Design
Rebecca Gradisek, gradisekdesigns.com

Illustrations
Diana Chan

Photography
Diana Chan, Godfrey Fong, Yao Gene Chan

Printing
Printed in China through Overseas Printing Corporation.

ISBN 978-1-4243-1960-2

Copyright © 2006
Diana Chan, Easy 'n Healthy Publishers

Library of Congress Catalogue Card Number: 2007900443

www.easyandhealthycooking.com
easyandhealthycooking@yahoo.com

Foreword

It is my pleasure to recommend this cookbook. As the owner of Chef Chu's, I am always looking for innovative recipes that appeal to a wide variety of contemporary tastes. Diana Chan has shared her best recipes in this excellent collection of Chinese, Western and Fusion dishes that emphasize fresh ingredients and low-fat preparations.

Diana has included delicious Chinese soups and simple entrées that can be made in 30 minutes. These will appeal to busy homemakers and professionals who don't have time during the week to prepare elaborate meals. There are also gourmet recipes which take a little more time but are not hard to make.

You will find many new ideas for entertaining at home with ease and style. I have tasted several of the dishes included here from fusion appetizers such as Vietnamese Style Spring Rolls, to Chinese entrées like Wintermelon Vegetarian Gourmet, Shrimp with Soy Beans, and Tofu with Crab Roe, to dazzling Fusion entrées such as Filet Mignon with Chestnuts en Croûte, Medallion Chicken, and Sesame Encrusted Ahi Tuna. The desserts range from fruit tortes to easy and elegant cakes. I know you will enjoy preparing them for your family and guests.

Diana suggests many variations on her central themes, which translate into myriad ways of presenting food once a master recipe is learned. This book is an appealing new source for healthy, innovative, uncomplicated cooking. Enjoy!

Lawrence Chu
Los Altos, CA

Easy 'n Healthy Cooking
Chinese, Fusion, and Western Cuisine

This book is dedicated to my mother and late father, who imparted to me their love of fresh healthy food, simply prepared and attractively presented. The cookbook's emphasis on healthy cooking is attributed to my mother's keen interest in nutritional balance using lean meats, fresh vegetables, fruits, and very little oil.

Introduction

When my son and daughter-in-law wanted to learn Chinese cooking, I put together a few recipes and showed them the basics. It was a fun experience for all of us, and to my great surprise, they started making the dishes and soon were asking for more recipes. That is the genesis of this cookbook, with Easy and Healthy recipes that appeal to people who don't want to spend a lot of time in the kitchen.

As a child growing up in Shanghai and Hong Kong, I never went to the kitchen, for kids would just get in the way of busy adults. When our family moved to Brazil, I started watching our Chinese cook, a very talented chef who could make dim sum and elaborate banquet dishes. He skillfully used two cleavers, like a drummer beating rhythmic patterns, when he chopped and minced meats into pâte. It was fun watching him, and that's how I learned the basics of Chinese cooking which facilitated my transition into Fusion cooking later on.

People often think of Chinese cooking as difficult and complicated, when in fact it's merely a matter of having the interest and the willingness to try a different method of cooking. I introduce many variations to several themes which translate into different ways of presenting dishes once a master recipe is learned. I have companion dishes which can be made the next day once the ingredients for an entrée are prepared, so that the next day's light meal requires just 5-10 minutes of assembling to create a brand new dish. This method makes meal preparation really easy, healthy, and interesting because one can enjoy foods presented in myriad ways with minimal effort.

While using traditional methods of Chinese cooking, I make a deliberate effort to cut down the use of oil in stir-frying and avoid deep frying altogether. I use a lot of vegetables with lean meats and seafood which give a healthy nutritional balance. I use the same nutritional and health-conscious philosophy when it comes to Western cuisine using lots of whole wheat flour, very little sugar, and lots of fresh fruit in many of the desserts. I measure meticulously when baking, but rely much more on my eyes, nose, and taste buds when it comes to cooking other dishes.

When I have dinner guests, menu planning often includes a mix of hot or cold Chinese and Western appetizers. Chinese dinners usually include more than one dish and they can be steamed, braised, or stir-fried. I favor make-ahead Western desserts. So the menu is quite eclectic, as Chinese food blends well with Western cuisine. For this reason, I have included Chinese, fusion, and Western recipes. I like to surprise friends with innovative ways of fusing Asian ingredients into Continental cuisine, as in the Filet Mignon with Chestnuts en Croûte and Medallion Chicken with Jeweled Rice en Croûte. Baked in a crust, these entrées look dazzling and seem to appeal to cosmopolitan tastes.

The reader can use the section on **Garnish, Ingredients and Cooking Tips** as a quick reference for a specific preparation or cutting method. The short paragraphs on **Basic Cutting and Cooking Methods in Chinese Cuisine** will be especially helpful to novices. Some of the recipes have a long list of ingredients, some of which require advanced soaking or preparation, but they are easily tossed together in the wok at the last minute with terrific end results. The **Easy and Delicious** recipes are **highlighted in bold letters**. It's a good idea to start by making the **Easy and Delicious** and **Easy Gourmet** recipes first to build confidence. The reader-cook is bound to make these dishes over and over again and will soon build a repertoire of favorites. There are many **gourmet** II recipes which will appeal to experienced cooks who want to make deliciously impressive entrées and appetizers. These may take a little more time but are surprisingly easy to make. There are many vegetarian and seafood dishes that are tasty, colorful, and nutritious. The **Vegetarian recipes** and the ones that have particularly healthy ingredients appealing to health conscious eaters are marked with ♥ hearts. The desserts range from low calorie and healthy to rich and irresistible. A theme throughout is the importance of eye appeal and presentation as well as great taste.

Cooking and baking are enjoyable pastimes as I play with recipes and create something new through experimentation. It's fun figuring out how to make a dish after trying it in a restaurant. My family and friends have been sampling my cooking and encouraging me throughout the years. Good food is a universal language. I hope you will have fun trying some of these recipes; many of them are amazingly simple to make, even for first timers.

Cover Photos
Crab Tsiu Chou Style, Shrimp with Soy Beans,
Wintermelon Vegetarian Gourmet, Vegetable Rice Shanghai Style in the electric rice cooker.
Desserts: Rum Cake, Apple Torte, Bavarian Mousse in a rose Bundt pan, and a mini Bavarian Mousse.
Top left insert: Crabmeat Fruit Salad. Right insert: Filet Mignon with Chestnuts en Croûte.
Back Cover Photo : Sesame Encrusted Ahi Tuna, Abalone King Mushrooms with Chinese Mustard Greens.

Acknowledgements

I am most grateful to S.K. and Angela Chan for their generous sponsorship of the cookbook and their belief in my style of easy and healthy cooking. I thank my husband for translating the names of the recipes into Chinese, for critiquing the food, and suggesting improvements. He is my technical advisor and gives me indispensable computer support. I am thankful to my sisters, Elizabeth and Lily, and friends Debbie Pao, Mary Chiu, Nancy Enomoto, Marina Yao, Lynn Jacob, Susan Steinberg, Louise Yu, and Tessie Teodoro who generously shared some of their recipes. I greatly appreciate Mabel Lai's generosity in sharing her expertise on cooking and two of her favorite recipes. Mabel, Flora Zee, and many relatives tested my recipes. I am grateful to my brother David, my daughter Stephanie, and my friend Helen Hubbs for the arduous first round of proof reading and recipe testing. I want to thank my sister-in-law, Susan Fong who spent much time editing and proof reading all the recipes and the manuscript. I appreciate the help from John Lee, George Shao, Paige Sachs, Joan Barr, Bob Oaks and Le Tran-Thi. I appreciate the help and suggestions in photography from Godfrey Fong and nephew, Yao Gene. I appreciate the help in proof reading from my fellow docent trainees, Carol Harlow, Bianca Larson, Yvonne Cheng, Maureen Poon, and my friend Lillian Chantalat. My son Derek gave me good legal advice and encouraged me to write the cookbook. I want to thank my niece, Angelina Chan, and some special friends, Antonia Tu, Debbie Pao, Emily Cheng, Ruth and Lawrence Chu, the owners of Chef Chu's, and Martin Yan who pointed me in the right direction and offered me their support.

What luck I had in finding Rebecca Gradisek, a young talented graphic designer to do the layout for the cookbook. She is creative, and supremely responsive to client requests. I am grateful to her for her gift and artistry as she translated my dream of writing this cookbook into reality. Many thanks to Lee Kum Kee for donating the cooking sauces that will be featured at the book signings.

Cooking for me is a creative expression which touches the lives of relatives and friends. Without their encouragement and support, I could not have undertaken this project.

TABLE OF CONTENTS

CHINESE CUISINE

FUSION & WESTERN CUISINE

Garnish Making

1. 4 carved columns of baby carrots
2. 1 carved column of white turnip
3. Cut carrot flowers
4. Cut white turnip flowers with green soybean centers
5. Peeled whole persimmon with scored ww cuttings
6. Split scored whole persimmon into 2 halves or 2 persimmon flowers
7. Persimmon peels being rolled into round concentric shape. Use left hand to hold the partially rolled peel, and right hand to curl the remaining peel into the shape of a rose.
8. Far right corner: Rolled persimmon peel that is ready to be turned over into a rose.
9. Bottom: Finished Persimmon Rose that is turned over & decorated with spinach leaves. Tomato Rose is made the same way as the Persimmon Rose.
   Peels of firm nectarines or white nectarines can also be made into flowers the same way.

Garnish, and Ingredients

Making Garnish

Garnish adds a finishing touch to dishes, making them beautiful, colorful, and elegant.

Tomato Rose
Use a sharp paring knife to peel a firm tomato, in one long piece starting at the narrow end on the bottom of tomato, as if you are peeling an apple. After peeling, begin at the stem end of the long peel and start curling it into a round spiral, being careful not to break the peel. Once finished, turn the spiral upside down, tighten the peel towards the bottom to create the shape of a rose bud and you have a beautiful tomato rose. Put the tomato rose on a small leaf from the heart of a green leaf or romaine lettuce. The lettuce keeps the rose in shape and creates color contrast. See Photo on Garnish Making.

Tomato or Persimmon Star After peeling the tomato skin for the Tomato Rose, take the peeled tomato and make continuous w-shaped cuts from the outside into the middle of the tomato all the way around. Then split the tomato apart along the W-shaped cuts, and you have two carved Tomato Stars. See Photo on Garnish Making.

Persimmon Rose Fuyu is a persimmon that can be peeled and eaten like an apple. Pick a firm fuyu that is not too ripe and use a paring knife to trim away the top stem leaf. Then follow the same procedure to cut the peel as in the Tomato Rose above and you have a pretty Persimmon Rose. See Photo on Garnish Making.

Carrot Flowers Peel the carrot and carve out 4-5 vertical notches lengthwise around the carrot. Then cut the carrot horizontally into thin slices of carved flowers. See Photo.

Beet Hearts & Butterflies Draw or trace a heart and butterfly on an index card. Cut it out as a mold, and trim the cooked, sliced beet to the paper mold.

Parsley and Green Leaf Lettuce make colorful liners around large platters of food.

Bok Choy Heart Centers have dainty yellow flowers. Trim the 1–2-inch heart tips for garnish. **Broccoli Florets** make the easiest garnish. Trim 1-inch florets.

Turnip with Soy Bean Centers Choose a white Chinese turnip that is 2 inches in diameter and straight like a column. Peel the turnip, cut it in half or thirds and cook in chicken broth for 30-40 minutes until it is tender. Remove from broth and cool.

Carve out five shallow vertical notches lengthwise around the turnip, giving it the shape of a six-petal flower. Cut or core out a third inch center in the middle of the turnip from top to bottom for stuffing.
Cut turnip into 1/2-inch horizontal slices and stuff a green soybean or cooked pea sprouts in the middle of the sliced turnip. **See photos of Garnish Making.**

Cooking Tips: Basic Cooking Methods in Chinese Cuisine

鑊氣 **Wok Hay** translated as "**breath of the wok**" is a very important concept in Chinese cooking in the stir-fry method described below. Chinese restaurants use extremely powerful gas burners.
Most homes are not equipped with that type of range. To compensate for the lower BTU used in home ranges, it is crucial to heat the dry wok to a very high temperature **before** adding oil. If all the ingredients are ready, and the food is stir-fried at the right temperature, with the right amount of oil, and served piping hot, the dish has "wok hay" because the juice of the meat and vegetables are sealed into the food making it very palatable.

Stir-Frying A basic principle of stir-frying is to heat the wok until it is very hot. You can see smoke coming out from the dry wok. Add oil, swirl oil, and stir-fry by continuously turning the food over with a spatula over high heat. It gives you the most efficient use of the hot wok, even if the range is not as powerful as you would like it to be. The oil is just hot enough to quickly cook the meat without burning it. As you continue stir-frying, add a little chicken broth (1Tbsp,) mushroom water, or wine to the food and let the steam help cook the food with just enough juice to keep it moist and sizzling. Stir-frying is a very fast and efficient way of cooking.

Steaming Bring the water to a boil before putting in the dish for steaming. The dish sits on a rack in a pot, a wok, or large 12" frying pan which holds it steadily during the steaming without letting water spill into the dish. The covered pot with the dish steaming inside the pot is a healthy, low calorie way of cooking the food without oil while retaining the juice and natural flavor of the food. The timing of the steaming is more accurate when you put in the food after the water starts boiling. It is a traditonal way of cooking whole fish. Many meat and vegetarian dishes are steamed.

Braising is a slow way of cooking meats in a seasoned broth so that the liquid slowly evaporates and the juice is soaked into the food over a period of several hours until the food is tender and tasty. Always bring the entire contents of the pot to a boil when a new ingredient is added, then reduce the heat and let it cook on medium or low as specified in the recipe. Add liquid if needed as ranges vary and may require more or less liquid or time than indicated on recipe. If you want to reduce the liquid quickly when the food is tender, you could leave the lid of the pot open to increase the rate of evaporation. Braising is an easy way of letting the food cook slowly with minimal work and attention.

Microwaving is sometimes used to prepare vegetables in stir-fry dishes because it cuts down calories by not having to stir-fry the vegetables in oil first. The vegetables are combined with the rest of the stir-fried meats or seafood when they are half cooked thus saving time and effort without sacrificing taste and the presentation of fresh crisp vegetables. Place a piece of wax paper on top of the dish of vegetables so that it cooks quickly and evenly. Nutritionally, it is healthy to eat vegetables that are not overcooked with the vitamins and minerals not lost through cooking. Microwaves vary slightly in the amount of time needed for cooking.

Parboiling or Blanching is a way of prepping certain vegetables like mustard greens by boiling in chicken broth in some of the recipes so that the vegetable is half cooked and tenderized. Then the vegetable is strained and later tossed in with the rest of the meat or seafood. It is a way of prepping certain vegetables that require longer cooking time. The chicken broth is saved and used for broth or another blanching. Bean sprouts can be parboiled in boiling water and strained, to get rid of the extra water in the sprouts so that the main dish does not have too much liquid when combined with the bean sprouts. Chinese broccoli with the thick stems are parboiled in boiling water and a little baking soda to tenderize the heavy stems. Chinese broccoli does not have florets like Western broccoli. Western broccoli florets should never be treated with baking soda.

Deep Frying is hardly ever used in my recipes. It is one of my personal idiosyncrasies to find ways of circumventing the heavy use of oil for health and dietary preferences.

Cooking Tips: Cutting Methods used in Chinese Cuisine

Slicing It is easier to cut meats when they are half frozen. Costco has frozen chicken filet that are individually wrapped, skinned, and deboned, and ready to be sliced. Slice meats against the grain. e.g. The grain of the flank steak runs horizontally. So it is best to cut the flank steak into long strips of 11/2 inch width, then cut against the grain vertically into 1/8-inch slices.

Dicing For ease of handling, it is best to cut meats when it's half frozen. Cut into thin vertical slices and then into thin horizontal squares.

Cubing Cut meats when they are half frozen. The cubes are small 1/4 -1/2 inch pieces. Meats, and vegetables like bamboo shoots, pressed tofu, and mushrooms can be cubed.

Mincing It is much faster and easier to mince meats and vegetables in a food processor. Mince by hand chopping when using very small quantities of an ingredient.

Roll Cutting This method of cutting long cylindrical vegetables increases the cooking surface of the food.e.g. cut diagonally across the asparagus or carrot; roll the vegetable slightly, and make another 1-inch diagonal cut, continuing until the vegetable is cut into angular shapes. This method of cutting decreases the cooking time, enhances flavor absorption, and produces a pretty cut.

Tips on Buying Seafood

Selecting Fish

If live fish is available, it is far superior to fresh fish that are in the display case. The texture of fresh fish from the display case should be firm. Fresh fish should never be smelly; it should have no smell. Ask to have the fish cleaned and scaled at the market. Whole fish should be served with the head.

Selecting Shrimp

If you can buy frozen uncooked shrimp that is shelled and deveined, it is a big time saver. Otherwise, look for shrimp with white meat, rather than the pinkish variety. If the shrimp is defrosted in the display case, the body should be firm, not mushy.

Selecting Live Shellfish

Buy only live shellfish from the tank. Live clams always have closed shells.
If you are preparing crab, Chinese style, the fish market will prep and clean the crab for you. Always keep the shell. If you buy fresh abalone, it must be live from the tank.

Recipe Notations

Serving Sizes in the Chinese Cuisine section are estimated on serving Chinese dinners with multiple entrées. If you are trying out a single recipe as the only entrée for dinner, the serving size needs to be adjusted. Serving Sizes in the Western Cuisine section are based on a single entrée.

Easy and Delicious recipes are highlighted in bold letters for those who want to spend minimal time in cooking. Vegetarian and extra healthy recipes are notated with hearts ♥ in bold. Seasoned cooks will want to try some of the more elaborate recipes besides the easy and delicious ones. **Gourmet** entrées and desserts may take a little more time to prepare but are not hard to make. Do not be intimidated by the number of ingredients in some of the recipes. Most dry ingredients can be kept in the pantry for a long time and will be used in many different ways. Many dry ingredients are soaked in advance and tossed together in the wok for stir-fry dishes that can be done in a few minutes. The key to successful Chinese cooking is preparation. Read the recipe completely, and the section on Wok Hay, Stir-Frying, Companion Dishes, and Chinese Dry and Fresh Ingredients for Mushroom Preparation. It will save you time and help you get a good start on Chinese cooking.

Companion Dishes

Companion Dishes that can be prepared, cooked, steamed, or baked at the same time save a lot of time and effort. By doubling the ingredients, some of the desserts with similar bases can be made and frozen ahead of time. See Rum Cake, Lemon Poppy Seed Bread, the Heavenly Fruit Torte, and Low Calorie Trifle. The Vegetarian Goose and Steamed Vegetarian Rolls with similar ingredients are made and steamed simultaneously. The Vegetarian Goose can be frozen and used anytime you need an extra dish or appetizer.

Baked Crab in Shells and the Mariner's Crab Cakes make good companion dishes the following day because they use the same ingredients but are cooked differently.

The Sliced Chicken with Mushrooms & Bean Sprouts can be an entrée and also one of the main ingredients in the Vietnamese Style Spring Roll.

Companion Dishes are great time savers without sacrificing taste and variety. **See Rice and Noodles** section for more Companion Dishes.

Substitution of Ingredients

Substitution of Ingredients can often be made by either increasing the quantity of an accompanying ingredient or using a similar alternative ingredient. For example, if cloud ear mushrooms are not available, use more black mushrooms or a different fresh mushroom. Broccoli or Chinese mustard greens can be substituted for bok choy. **Soy milk** can sometimes be substituted for **whole milk**. **Pale dry sherry wine** can be substituted for **Shaoxing wine. corn starch** can be substituted for **tapioca starch.** Tapioca starch is lighter than corn starch. If you cannot get tapioca starch, found in Chinese supermarkets, then use corn starch. I prefer tapioca starch because it gives a light coating to meats without being too starchy.

Variations on a Theme

One of the most popular TV cooking shows features Rachel Ray as she prepares 30- minute meals using master recipes to spin off numerous dishes. I have been doing the same thing with my Chinese, Fusion, and Western dishes for years. Instead of using the term master recipe, I use the term variations on a theme, which translates into the creation of new entrées, desserts, and companion dishes based on a central theme.

In music and dance, composers and choreographers create beautiful variations on a theme. Beethoven wrote 32 Variations in C minor, Mozart wrote twelve variations on Twinkle, Twinkle, Little Star. George Balanchine choreographed ballet vignettes using Tchaikovsky's Theme and Variations. Monet did several sequential paintings of Hay Stacks under different lighting.

Chefs and novice cooks can do the same by modifying a recipe while using the same theme for new creations. For example, the Winter Melon Vegetarian Gourmet is a variation of Buddha's Vegetarian Delight using simplified ingredients with totally new taste and presentation. Similarly, by adding a shellfish from Mexico and cutting out the bean curd, the simple OnChoy with Bean Curd becomes a new dish which looks and tastes like the prized abalone without the expense. The same holds true for the play on Vegetarian Goose, which spun off Steamed Vegetarian Rolls. These dishes have totally different personalities and taste, but are variations on the same theme.

My sister Lily got me started on the Salmon en Croûte which in turn inspired me to create three new entrées fusing favorite Chinese ingredients into Fusion and Continental entrées as in the Medallion Chicken with Chestnuts en Croûte, Medallion Chicken with Jeweled Rice en Croûte, and Filet Mignon with Chestnuts en Croûte. The first two entrées taste and look so different from their Chinese cousins that they belong to the Fusion and Continental Cuisine section rather than the Chinese Cuisine.

The noodles recipes can have many more variations by using the same methods with different vegetables, seafoods, and meats or all vegetarian ingredients for noodle toppings. This creates fast, easy companion dishes. The stir-fry recipes have lots more variations depending on what you see in the market for fresh vegetables. The meats are prepared and marinated in the same way while you cook the vegetables using one of the three simple methods in the Chinese section. Then toss the vegetables into the wok with the main ingredients when the food is almost done.

I've been having a lot of fun creating new dishes without realizing half the time that I've been developing variations on different themes. You should try this sometime. Once you get familiar with a recipe and how it tastes, don't be afraid to vary the recipe, add, delete, or substitute ingredients. By experimenting with what you do, you will be surprised how much fun cooking can be, and how you might come upon new creations.

Dry and Fresh Chinese Ingredients

1. Pkg Mushroom Seasoning
2. Pkg Dried Cloud Ear Mushroom
3. Canned Abalone from Australia
4. Canned Top Shellfish from Mexico
5. Hwa Tiao Wine
6. Shaoxing Wine
7. Oyster Sauce
8. Crab Paste
9. Wet Bean Curd
10. Canned Fried Gluten
11. Canned Straw Mushrooms
12. Dried Bamboo Pith
13. Dried White Back Black Mushrooms
14. Dried Cloud Ear Mushroom from Pkg
15. Dried Black Mushroom
16. Pkg Dried Scallops
17. Dried Abalone from Australia
18. Star Anise
19. Dried Peppercorn
20. Fresh Frozen Gingko Nut

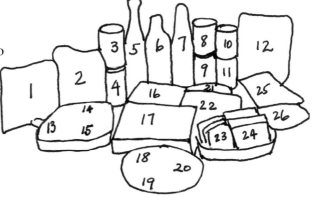

21. Mung Bean Vermicelli
22. Prosperity Vegetable
23. Marinated Pressed Tofu
24. Pressed Tofu
25. Dried Shrimp
26. Frozen Pkg Bean Sheets for Vegetarian Goose and Vegetarain Rolls

17

Chinese Dry and Fresh Ingredients, Mushroom Preparation

Dried Black Mushrooms 冬菇 are one of the most frequently used ingredients in Chinese cooking. They should be kept in a tightly sealed container. The thick variety with flowery veins on the cap is very fragrant. Presoak some black mushrooms in water for 4 hours or overnight and keep them refrigerated as they are used in many Chinese dishes. Save the fragrant soaking water to add flavor to the food and use according to recipes

Cloud Ear Mushrooms 雲耳 expand to 5 times their volume. If you get a premium brand with dainty petals like the kind in the photo, there is less time spent changing the water during the soaking. Keep changing the water used to soak the mushrooms until the water is clear. Discard the water used to soak this mushroom. Discard the black, hard stem ends. The Cloud Ear Mushrooms are used in many of my recipes because they add a crunchy texture, and interesting color contrast to the food. Presoak and clean the mushrooms days ahead of time as they can be refrigerated for many days and are so frequently used in many vegetarian, meat, and seafood dishes.

White Back Black Wood Ear Mushroom 白背黑木耳 is the exact translation of this mushroom. The Chinese believe it helps reduce cholesterol. The dried mushroom is white on one side, and black on the other and expands to eight times its volume when soaked in water; discard the hard stem ends and change water until it's clear. Slice the mushrooms and cook in chicken broth on low for about 2-3 hrs until most of the broth gets absorbed and evaporated. It could be used in soups or any dish that calls for cloud ear mushrooms. This mushroom can be found at a specialty seafood and herbal chain store called Chung Chou City 蟲草城.

Dried Straw Mushrooms 干草菇 are the most fragrant of mushrooms. Keep a package in a sealed container. 1/4 cup of straw mushrooms soaked in water will add tremendous flavor and fragrance to food. Wash straw mushrooms carefully and scrape off all the sand that is stuck to the mushrooms. Rinse several times in clear water to make sure there are no remnants of sand. Filter straw mushroom water through a coffee filter or paper towel and use the fragrant water in cooking. Cleaned straw mushrooms keep well in the refrigerator.

Mushroom Seasoning 香菇顆粒調味料 is sometimes used because it adds flavor to the food without MSG. It can be used sparingly in soups and vegetables at about 1tsp for 1 cup of water, or 1/2 -1 tsp for 4 cups of vegetables while stir-frying. Reduce salt and other seasoning if you are using mushroom seasoning. It's a great substitute for chicken broth for strict vegetarian cooking. See photo on p. 17.

Prosperity Vegetable 發菜 is a vegetable eaten during the Chinese New Year celebration because the name puns with "prosperity." It is a vegetable used in many vegetarian dishes. Preparation: Soak a small handful in water and it expands. The vegetable needs to be rinsed several times until the water is clear. Sauté prosperity vegetable in some oil before using it in a dish.

Lotus Seeds 蓮子 a fresh vegetable found in the refrigerated section, vacuum packed. It is often eaten during Chinese New Year as it puns with "consecutive sons." Some vegetarian dishes and desserts use this ingredient.

Gingko Nut 白果 is a nut used in vegetarian dishes, as the lotus seeds.

Fresh Bean Sheets 鮮腐皮 are used to make vegetarian goose and vegetarian rolls. They come in large 26" round sheets and are found in the frozen food section.

Fresh Bean Bao 腐包 made from soy beans are used to make vegetarian dishes. They are found in the refrigerated section of large Chinese supermarkets.

Fresh or Frozen Bean Curd Knots 百頁結 made from soy beans are used in meat and vegetarian dishes and soups, popular in the Shanghai style of cooking. They are found in the refrigerated section of large Chinese supermarkets.

Vermicelli 粉絲 are thin white bean threads that look like transparent noodles Soak a small package in water and it will soften. It is used in many meat and vegetarian dishes.

Tiger Lily 金針 is a dry ingredient used in many vegetarian dishes. I deliberately delete this ingredient because it takes a long time to prep it. Due to the dry pollens embedded inside the stems, I find it too time consuming to clean and prep, to cut open the stems, to discard the pollens (which leave a yellowish stain on the skin.) and trim the hard stems.

Bamboo Pith 竹笙 is the delicate center of bamboo used in soups and vegetables. Soak the dried bamboo pith in water, changing the water until it is clear. A tablespoon of salt will help get rid of some of the yellow color. Rinse in cold water again.

Dried Shrimp 蝦米 is used to add flavor to meat and vegetable. Keep a couple of those packages handy. Store dried shrimp in a tightly sealed container.

Dried Scallops 干貝(干瑤柱)are expensive but a few soaked in water add much flavor to food. Always save the fragrant water used to soak the scallops for cooking.

Sea Cucumbers 海參 are used in soups or braised dishes. The small frozen ones are best. Parboil in cold water, and rinse thoroughly before simmering in soup or a sauce. It's one of the ingredients in Buddha Jumps the Wall, a delicious soup.

Dried Fish Maw 魚膠 are available in large or small size. The large ones are expensive but easier to use. Soak fish maw in water for several days; change the water many times until the color of the fish maw turns to white. Small fish maw need to be soaked for several days and cleaned to get rid of sand. Parboil in water, rinse thoroughly and simmer in chicken broth for soup. It's one of the ingredients in Buddha Jumps the Wall, a delicious soup.

Dried Bamboo 鹹筍 are salted and used to make prime chicken broth; they are also used in some meat dishes.

Spices: Star Anise 八角 adds fragrance to braised and baked foods.

Peppercorn 花椒 adds fragrance to braised and baked foods.

White Pepper 白胡椒 is used in preference to black pepper.

Salted Black Beans 豆豉 enhance flavor in vegetables and meats.

Soy Bean Paste 豆瓣醬 adds flavor to meats and vegetables.

Preserved Bean Curd 腐乳 is often served with plain rice porridge.

Preserved Mustard Green 梅菜 is used in some of the meat dishes.

Salted Mustard Green 雪菜 is used in some of the recipes.

Crab Paste with Soy Bean Oil adds flavor and color to foods and is used in some of my tofu recipes. **See Photo p 17.**

Dried Vietnamese Spring Roll Skin, sometimes called **Tapioca Sheets or Rice Paper Wrappers** in round packages are used for the Vietnamese Style Spring Rolls. They are thin translucent sheets about 9 or 10 inches in diameter. **See Photo p. 110.**

Dark Soy Sauce is used primarily to give a rich color to braised meats so that they have a desired glaze. Lee Kum Kee has a Premiium Dark Soy Sauce and Mushroom Flavored Dark Soy Sauce.

Light Soy Sauce is used to add taste to meats and vegetables. Kikkoman can be used as either light or dark soy sauce.

Double Deluxe Soy Sauce is a dipping sauce or flavorful sauce by Lee Kum Kee added at the end of some stir-fry dishes.

Soy Sauce Paste 醬油膏 is a dark sauce used for braising meats to create a dark shimmering sauce for Shanghainese cooking.

Oyster Sauce is used to add flavor to meats and vegetables. It is often used when the foods are ready to be seasoned to taste. A premium brand of oyster sauce is preferred.

Vegetarian Stir-Fry Sauce 素食蠔油 by Lee Kum Kee is similar to oyster sauce that adds flavor to vegetarian foods.

Tapioca Starch 太白粉 **or Corn Starch** is used to coat meats and shellfish before stir frying. Tapioca starch is also used to thicken gravy. Tapioca starch can be found in Chinese supermarkets. If tapioca starch is not available, use cornstarch.

Crab Tsiu Chou Style

Chinese Cuisine
Hot and Cold Appetizers

Parboiled Live Shrimp
Crab Tsiu Chou Style
Spinach with Peanut Sauce
Asparagus with Wasabi Dip
Fresh Soy Beans in Pods

Pressed Tofu with Chives
Sea Jelly Fish
Grilled Chicken Livers
Shrimp Medley
Steamed Empress Clams

Parboiled Live Shrimp 白灼蝦

1 lb of live, swimming shrimp or prawns
Basic Sauce: 2 Tbsp hot oil, 2 tsp light soy sauce, 1 1/2 tsp sugar
If a hot spicy flavor is desired, add 1 small red pepper cut into thin slices.

Heat a large pot of water to boil. Parboil prawns for 2 min or until the water boils again after the prawns are put in the pot. Small live shrimp will cook immediately in less than a minute. These prawns have to be cooked just the right amount of time, so that the meat is tender and succulent. If a small pot of water is used, the cooking time of the prawns will have to be increased, making the prawns less tender. The prawns will turn pink almost immediately when poured into the pot, and will be ready to be drained within a few minutes. Heat basic sauce in a small covered bowl and microwave for 1 minute on high. Drain prawns in a colander and serve immediately with heated basic sauce.

This makes a lavish **Easy and Delicious** first course. Small live shrimp from the tank are exceptionally tender. For the **gourmet**, the head of the prawn is the pièce de résistance.

Crab Tsiuzhou Style 潮州蟹

1 live Dungeness crab
4 14-oz cans chicken broth or 7 cups prime chicken broth*
8 cloves of fresh garlic, finely diced

Sauce: Soak diced garlic in 1/8 cup distilled white vinegar, 3 tsp sugar, & 4 tsp water. The ingredients can be adjusted to suit your taste for a milder or stronger sauce.

Live crab is needed for this recipe, not fresh dead crab. Ask the store where you buy the live crab to open the shell of the crab and clean it. Keep the shell and the crab roe.
Use a deep pot to bring the chicken broth or basic stock or mushroom water to a boil. The broth should cover the crab and shell entirely. Put the crab in the boiling broth and cook for 5-6 min. on medium until it boils; reduce heat and cook on low for 5 min. Do not open the lid of the pot. Leave the pot covered until completely cool. Then cut crab into 4-6 pieces and arrange into its original form with the shell on top. Place crab on a serving plate. Refrigerate. Serve cold with vinegar sauce. This makes an **Easy and Delicious** cold appetizer or first course.

*Note: An easy timesaving shortcut to chicken broth is to make a broth of 1 tsp Mushroom Seasoning per 1 cup water. Mushroom Seasoning does not have MSG.
See Dry Ingredients p 17.

♥ Spinach with Peanut Sauce

2 cups pre-washed spinach
3 Tbsp peanut butter
Light soy sauce, Sugar

Microwave spinach for 1 minute until leaves are limp. Squeeze spinach in between 2 plates to get rid of excess water.
Mix 3Tbsp peanut butter, with a little soy sauce and sugar to taste. Mix the sauce with spinach.
Fill a rice bowl with the spinach mixture, pack, and invert onto a serving plate.
Serve spinach cold. It's an **Easy, Healthy and Delicious** vegetarian side dish.

♥ Asparagus with Wasabi Dip

1 bunch of fresh asparagus
2 Tbsp light mayonnaise

light soy sauce
A dash of wasabi

Use the tender 4 inch tips of the asparagus only. Save the rest of the stems for vegetables.
Wash asparagus, cover and microwave for 11/2 minute. Asparagus should be barely cooked and slightly crunchy. Some microwaves may require more time (11/2 -3 minutes.)
Mix mayonnaise with a little soy sauce and wasabi to taste.
Serve asparagus with wasabi dip.
It's a delightfully **Easy, Healthy and Delicious** cold appetizer that can be made ahead of time.

♥ Fresh Soybeans in Pods

1 package of fresh frozen soy beans in pods, parboiled in water.
Drain and sauté in 3Tbsp of Lee Kum Kee Drunken Chicken Marinade for a few minutes.
Drain and serve hot or cold as an appetizer.
It's a refreshingly **Easy, Healthy and Delicious** vegetarian appetizer.

♥ Pressed Tofu with Chives

2 pieces of pressed tofu
1/2 bunch of chives
Salt, sugar, Oyster sauce
Pure sesame seed oil

Parboil pressed tofu and chives in chicken broth. Dice tofu into 1/8 inch cubes. Cut chives into small 1/8 inch pieces. Mix salt and a little oyster sauce with the diced pressed tofu and chives. Season to taste with salt, sugar, and a dash of sesame seed oil. It's an **Easy, Healthy and Delicious** side dish that is served cold.

♥ Sea Jelly Fish 海哲

1 pkg jelly fish (found in the refrigerated section of Chinese supermarkets)
Sauce: 2Tbsp oil with 1Tbsp light soy sauce or oyster sauce, 1 1/2 tsp sugar, sesame seed oil

Soak the sheets of sea jellyfish in cold water. Rinse and change water several times a day, getting rid of the salt and sand. Soaking it overnight or several days ahead helps get rid of the salt and sand. When the water comes out clear, with no sand, it is ready for preparation.

Cut the jelly fish sheets into 1/8" x 2" thin slices.
Pour a large pot of boiling water over the jelly fish in a strainer.
Immediately dunk the sliced jelly fish in icy cold water so that it becomes crunchy.
Heat basic sauce, let cool, then mix with sliced and drained jelly fish. Add a dash of sesame oil just before serving for fragrance. It's a refreshing and **Healthy** cold appetizer.

Jelly fish is low in calories and full of rich minerals, especially iodine; jelly fish is good for the thyroid. A fresh package keeps in the refrigerator for a long time.

Grilled Chicken Liver 金錢雞

1/4 lb chicken livers, cut into 1/2 inch pieces
1/2 chicken breast, cut against the grain into 1 inch slices
A few slices of lean bacon, sliced lengthwise first and cut into 2-inch pieces
1 stalk scallion, cut, 3 cloves garlic, sliced
2 tsp soy sauce, 1 1/2 tsp honey
1 tsp Shaoxing cooking wine or pale dry sherry
Toothpicks

Marinate chicken livers, sliced chicken breast, scallions, garlic, wine, and honey for at least an hour or overnight. Use a toothpick to skewer the ingredients like a club sandwich: bacon, sliced chicken, bacon, chicken liver, bacon. Broil on low for 10-15 minutes until lightly brown as in a barbecue, turning toothpick skewers over once. This appetizer should be served hot.

Shrimp Medley 蝦仁生菜包

1/2 lb shrimp, cleaned, deveined, and diced into 1/4 inch pieces
6 black mushrooms, presoaked overnight, and diced into 1/4 inch pieces
3/4 cup winter bamboo shoots, diced into 1/4 inch pieces (optional)
3/4 cup fresh, frozen, or canned whole corn kernels
3/4 cup frozen peas, defrosted
1/4 cup toasted pine nuts (optional)
Iceberg lettuce, cut into the shape of 5-inch scallop shells
2 stalks scallions, diced
1 1/2 tsp cornstarch
1 tsp oyster sauce, 2 Tbsp oil
3 cloves garlic, minced
Salt, white pepper, sugar
1 Tbsp Shaoxing wine or pale dry sherry

Buy small, uncooked, shelled and deveined shrimp if available to save time in prepping. Otherwise, get the large shrimp; shell and devein shrimp in cold water and 1 tsp salt. Salt improves the texture of the shrimp. Rinse in cold water, drain, dry shrimp with paper towel, and cut shrimp into 1/4 inch pieces. Mix cornstarch, salt and white pepper with shrimp. Set aside.

Carefully remove the outer layers of iceberg. Cut the end stem piece. Carefully unwrap the layers of lettuce and use scissors to trim each leaf into a scallop shaped 5-inch cup. Save the lettuce trimmings for salads. Refrigerate lettuce cups.

Heat wok on high, add 2 Tbsp oil. Stir-fry shrimp, garlic, mushrooms. Season with salt, white pepper, wine, and a little sugar. When it's almost cooked, add corn, peas, scallions, and winter bamboo shoots. Stir-fry everything 1-2 minutes, depending on the power of the range. Season to taste. Sprinkle some pine nuts on the shrimp medley.

Serve with lettuce cups as a hot appetizer or serve alone as a seafood entrée. This is an **Easy and Delicious** recipe which can be prepared quickly, if you have all the ingredients ready.

Steamed Empress Clams 貴妃蚌

2 Giant Clams, live from the tank
3 stalks scallions cut into 1 1/2 inch slivers
4 cloves garlic, minced
2 Tbsp Shaoxing wine or pale dry sherry
Salt, white pepper
1 tsp light soy sauce
2 Tbsp oil

Have the giant clams opened, meat removed and cleaned at the seafood market. Keep the shells. Wash and scrub the shells.

Thoroughly clean the clam meat several times, making sure there is no sand left in any of the pockets of the clams. This is crucial, because no matter how delicious the steamed clams may be, if there are bits of sand left in the clams, they will not taste good.

Put half shells on serving dish with meat of clams (cut to 1/4" slices), spread evenly on top of shells.

Sprinkle a little soy sauce, wine, garlic, and half of the scallions on clams.

Bring water to a boil in a steamer. Then put in seasoned clams and steam in a covered pot on high for 2 minutes. Check to see if clams are done. Do not over steam as clams will toughen.

Drizzle hot vegetable oil on steamed clams.

Serve immediately. Serves 4. Each empress clam serves 2.

I have also microwaved the clams instead of steaming them. Microwave seasoned clams on high for 1-2 minutes, depending on the microwave. Pour hot oil over cooked clams.

This makes a delicious gourmet hot appetizer or first course. If well prepped, and steamed with just the right timing, the Steamed Empress Clams are truly la pièce de résistance.

Steamed Poached Sea Bass with Rice Porridge

Seafood Entrées

Scallops with Asparagus
Emerald Braised Abalone
Shellfish with Mustard Greens
Baked Crab with Rice Porridge
Steam Poached Sea Bass Filet
Fish Fillet with Vinegar Sauce
Steamed Fish
Wok Seared Prawns

Crab Roe with Tofu
Stuffed Melon with Shrimp
Shrimp with Soy Beans
Shrimp Stuffed Tofu
Seafood with Steamed Tofu
Shrimp Stuffed Egg Plants
Slivered Pressed Tofu with Shrimp

29

Scallops with Asparagus
蘆筍帶子

3/4 lb fresh scallops (about 12 large scallops)
3 cloves of garlic, 3 Tbsp tempura batter mix
3/4 lb fresh asparagus or sugar pea pods
3 Tbsp oil, Salt, white pepper, sugar

Use the juice (about 2 Tbsp) from the package of fresh scallops to mix with 3 Tbsp tempura batter until the batter is of the consistency of a thick pancake mix. Add scallops and let it sit in the batter. Set aside. (The juice from the scallop is very tasty.)

Break asparagus where the stem naturally snaps. Wash the tender asparagus spears, then microwave on high for 1 1/2 minutes or until 85% cooked, but still crunchy.

Cover asparagus with a piece of wax paper when microwaving so that it cooks quickly and evenly.

Heat wok until it's very hot; add 3 Tbsp oil, swirl oil, and stir-fry scallops and garlic until the scallops are lightly coated and barely cooked. If you are using a small wok, try stir-frying scallops in two batches or cook a smaller amount with more vegetables. Do not over cook, as scallops toughen if overcooked. Add asparagus, and season to taste with salt, pepper, a little cooking wine, and 1 tsp sugar. Stir-fry another minute until scallops are done and serve immediately.

The wok-seared scallops are tender and succulent. This is an **Easy and Delicious gourmet** seafood entrée. Serves 4-6.

30

Emerald Braised Abalone 碧綠鮑片

3 live abalone from the tank (choose large ones)
Fresh mustard green
8 large black mushrooms, presoaked for 4 hrs or overnight
3 cloves garlic
1 tsp light soy sauce
1/2 tsp Lee Kum Kee double deluxe soy sauce (optional)
Oyster sauce
1Tbsp Shaoxing wine or pale dry sherry
2 cups chicken broth
1 star anise
1 piece of raw sugar (about 1 Tbsp)

Depending on the size of the abalone, 3 large ones weighing 3 lbs should serve 10.
Have the abalone shelled at the seafood market. Bring abalone to a boil with 4 cups of water, garlic, soy sauces, wine and star anise, making sure the water level covers the abalone completely. Cover the pot and simmer 5-6 hrs. Be sure there is enough water to keep it simmering. During the last 45 minutes, add whole black mushrooms, with stems removed. Continue simmering. Reduce the water level to about 3/4 cup at the end of the five hours. Abalone should be tender and the juice has a light brown color. Remove star anise. Let cool.

Slice abalone across the width of the body, keeping the slices as whole and as thin as possible. I use a Krups electric slicer to get the thin slices.

Take the center or the heart of the mustard green, or small leaves. Bring 2 cups of chicken broth to a boil and cook the mustard green, leaving the lid open until you can easily pierce the stem with a chopstick. (about 2-3 minutes) The vegetable stays bright green as long as you don't cover the lid. Drain vegetable.

Melt the raw sugar in the remaining juice of the abalone, giving it a shiny glaze. Season to taste with a little oyster sauce, and simmer the abalone for 15 minutes before serving. Pour the juice over sliced abalone, whole mushrooms, and parboiled mustard green. Braised abalone is a feast dish and a prized seafood relished by **gourmets.**

shellfish with Chinese Mustard Green 鮑片扒芥菜膽

1 can of Top Shellfish (from Mexico)
1 bunch fresh Chinese mustard green or Chinese broccoli
A pinch of baking soda, 1 tsp salt
5 cloves garlic, sliced
1 Tbsp vegetable oil

This is a discovery that I made recently when I bought a can of Top Shellfish from Mexico at the Chinese grocery store. The taste and texture is similar to abalone and when sliced, it looks like abalone. You have to try it to appreciate it. The price of the shellfish is a fraction of abalone, so it is well worth the effort to sample this seafood.

Place shellfish flat on the cutting board, and slice horizontally to thin pieces.
Parboil Chinese mustard green or bok choy in a large pot of boiling water with baking soda and 1 tsp salt until the stems are tender but not soggy (barely 30 seconds.) Baking soda tenderizes the vegetable and keeps it green. Don't use Western broccoli with baking soda. Drain.

Sauté green vegetable in a little oil and juice from the can of shellfish and spread sliced shellfish on top of green vegetable. Season to taste and serve hot or cold. The juice from the shellfish is delicious and can be saved for cooking other vegetables or soups.

This is an **Easy and Delicious** seafood entrée for company or a family dinner!

Baked Crab with Rice Porridge
焗蟹燴飯

1 live Dungeness crab
8 Black mushrooms, presoaked 4 hrs or overnight in 2 cups cold water
1 1/2 cups of cooked rice,
4 cups of chicken broth
2 stalks scallions, slivered into 1 1/2 inch lengths
1 sheet of dry seaweed, cut into thin 1 1/2 inch slices (optional)
1 Tbsp pale dry sherry or Shaoxing cooking wine
Salt, white pepper, sesame oil (optional)
Heavy aluminum foil

Live crab is needed for this recipe, not fresh dead crab. Ask the store where you buy the live crab to open the shell of the crab and clean it. Keep the shell and crab roe intact. At home, cut the crab into 4 or 6 pieces, arrange the crab into its original form, and place it on a large sheet of heavy aluminum foil (18"x 28" depending on the size of the crab.) Sprinkle wine and a little chicken broth on the crabmeat. Put the shell back on the crab so that it looks like a whole crab.

Carefully fold the aluminum foil with the crab centered, and the closing of the foil crease on top. Now fold the two sides of the foil so it looks like a rectangular foil package. When folding the foil, **double fold the crease on top and the sides** so that the moisture is sealed in during the baking, and the crabmeat stays moist.

Discard mushroom stems, save mushroom water, and slice mushrooms into thin 1 1/2 inch slivers. Cook sliced mushrooms in chicken broth and 2 cups of mushroom water for 10 min. Season to taste.

Preheat oven to 500° and bake crab for 20 min. Cut the foil, leaving the top fold intact so that it serves as a handle, while peeling the foil back to the sides to form a "basket." Serve immediately. Serves 4-6 depending on the size of the crab.

Bring the chicken and mushroom broth to a boil with the cooked rice and wine; cook on medium for 5 min and add remaining slivered scallions, seaweed, sesame oil, and the juice from the baked crab. Season to taste. Serve hot rice porridge with baked crab.

♥ Steam Poached Sea Bass Filet with Rice Porridge
清燉雪魚燴飯

1 1/2 lb Sea Bass Filet, about 1 1/2 inches thick
6 cloves of garlic
6 stalks scallions, slivered into 2 inch lengths
3 slices ginger, peeled and slivered (optional)
8 Black mushrooms, presoaked for 4 hrs or overnight
Save the fragrant mushroom water (2-3 cups)
4 cups chicken broth
1 1/2 cups cooked rice
1 sheet of dry seaweed, cut into 1 1/2 inch slices or small 1-inch squares (optional)
1 tsp Lee Kum Kee double deluxe soy sauce
Oyster sauce, salt, white pepper
2 Tbsp Shaoxing cooking wine or pale dry sherry
Dash of sesame oil, optional
Fresh Chinese parsley or 1 stalk of slivered scallions for garnish

Hot Broth Discard stems and cut presoaked black mushrooms into thin slices. Cook sliced mushrooms in 4 cups of chicken broth and 2-3 cups of mushroom water seasoned with salt, white pepper, double deluxe soy sauce, and oyster sauce to make a strong tasty broth.
Cook on medium for 15 minutes. Set aside.

Sauté garlic in 1Tbsp of oil for a few minutes until garlic is lightly brown. Sprinkle salt, pepper, and 1 Tbsp wine on all sides of Sea Bass filet. Line the bottom of a 2 1/4 inch deep dish with sliced garlic halves, sliced ginger and a few pieces of cut scallions; place fish filet on top of the sliced ingredients. Now put 1/2 of the sliced mushrooms, and a few more pieces of cut scallions horizontally on top of the fish filet. Set aside.

When you are almost ready to serve dinner, pour some of the **hot broth** into a dish to cover more than half of the thick Bass Filet. Place the dish on a rack in a pot of boiling water, being careful that the water will not spill into the fish dish. Cover the pot and steam-poach on high for about 8-10 minutes or until the fish is just ready when a wooden chopstick easily goes through it. Depending on the size and weight of the fish, you adjust the quantity of the chicken broth, and the time used for steam poaching. Do not overcook fish. Once cooked, pour out 3/4 of the fish broth into the rice porridge (see below). Garnish with Chinese parsley and serve fish steaming hot. **Serves 4**

While fish is being steamed, combine the cooked rice with the remaining chicken and mushroom broth, sliced mushrooms, and 1 Tbsp wine, and cook for 5 minutes. Add the fish broth, sliced scallions, sesame oil, and season to taste. Garnish with sliced seaweed, slivered scallions or Chinese parsley. Serve the hot rice porridge with fish.
See Photo on page 29.

The sea bass is tender and delicious served with a savory rice porridge. Yummmmy.

♥ Fish Filet *with* Vinegar Sauce 醋溜魚片

1/2 lb fish filet (Orange roughy, Halibut, Rock Cod, or thick sole)
3 cups sugar pea pods
2 Tbsp tapioca starch or 1 Tbsp cornstarch
salt, pepper, Sugar
2 tsp Shaoxing cooking wine, or pale dry sherry
2-3 Tbsp Hua Tiao wine
2 Tbsp white distilled vinegar
4-5 cloves garlic, sliced
3 stalks scallions, cut into 1 1/2 inch lengths
3 Tbsp oil

Rinse fish in cold water, then dry with paper towel. Cut the fish filet into 1 1/2 inch pieces and marinate with Shaoxing wine, tapioca starch or cornstarch, salt, & pepper. Set aside.

Remove tendrils from sugar pea pods; rinse in cold water, and drain. Microwave pea pods for 1 1/2 minutes and test. Microwave up to 1 1/2 minutes more, or until the vegetable is 80% done, but still crunchy. Depending on the microwave oven, you may or may not need to cook the second 1 1/2 minutes.

Heat wok until it's very hot. Pour oil in wok, swirl oil and stir fry on high the fish and garlic cloves. Add Hua Tiao wine and distilled vinegar, a little at a time, using the liquid and steam to cook the fish. Add cooked pea pods and scallions. Season to taste with salt, white pepper, and a tsp sugar. Serves 2-4. This is an **Easy and Delicious** seafood entrée.

While cooking in the wok, stir fry carefully so that the fish stays in whole chunks. Do not over stir. Fish filets cook quickly in just a few minutes.

Family Dinners

Steamed Fish 1, Crab Roe with Tofu 2, Wok Seared Shrimp 3,
Winter Melon Vegetarian Gourmet 4

Crab Roe with Tofu # 1
Stuffed Melon with
Shrimp #2
Chicken with Pressed Tofu
& Soy Beans #3

An Eclectic Dinner

The appetizers, soup, entrées and desserts are all made ahead of time.

Multiple choice of appetizers for the hostess to choose:
Sesame Encrusted Ahi Tuna # 1, served as cold hors d'oeuvres (oblong plate) or
Sesame Encrusted Ahi Tuna # 2, served as a cold appetizer at the table, or
Stuffed Prawn with Crabmeat # 3, served as an hot appetizer at the table

Bean Curd Knots with Soy Beans # 4
Braised Duck with chestnuts # 5
Steamed Chicken in Clay Pot Steamers # 6, serve right after hot or cold appetizer
Abalone King Mushrooms with Chinese Mustard Greens # 7

Coffee Mousse Torte # 8

♥ Steamed Fish 清蒸魚

Live whole fish is preferable, but filet of fish is okay if you choose the thick filet cuts like Orange Roughy, Sea Bass, Ling Cod, or Salmon.

1 whole fish (1 1/4 lb) Black Bass, Sea Bass, or Rock Cod
4-5 cloves sliced fresh garlic
Ginger, sliced and slivered (optional)
3-5 stalks scallions, sliced into 1 1/2 inch pieces (save half for garnish)
1 Tbsp pale dry sherry or ShaoHsing cooking wine
Basic Sauce: 2 Tbsp oil, 2 tsp light soy sauce, 1 tsp double deluxe soy sauce (optional,) 1 tsp sugar
A whole fish requires more sauce than filet of fish.

The whole fish should be scaled and cleaned at the market. At home you check to get rid of any remnant scales on the fish by running a knife against the direction of the scales. Rinse fish in cold water and pat dry with paper towel. Season with salt, white pepper, wine, and 1/2 Tbsp of the basic sauce.
Line the bottom of the dish with sliced garlic and scallions; place fish on top of the garlic and scallions, then put more garlic, ginger, and scallions on top of the fish.

Microwaving: Put a sheet of wax paper on top of the fish to prevent splattering. (This cooks the fish more evenly.) For a whole fish weighing less than 1 1/4 lb, cook 3 minutes on high in microwave. Turn the fish plate around. Garnish fish with thinly slivered scallions and pour remaining **Basic Sauce** on fish, and microwave another minute, covered.   Check to see if fish is done as microwaves cook differently, so adjust cooking time accordingly. Whole fish takes a longer time to cook than filet of fish. If a chopstick goes through the body of the fish with ease, it is done. Don't overcook fish.
The traditional way of cooking steamed fish is steaming. For the convenience of the cook, microwaving the fish is an acceptable alternative.

Traditional steaming: Prepare fish the same way with soy sauce and seasoning, but leave the oil out until the fish is steamed. Bring water to a boil in a large pot with a small rack to hold the fish dish. Steam fish on high (dish uncovered) for 8-15 minutes, depending on the size of the fish. Whole fish takes a longer time to cook than fish filet. When the fish is done, add more slivered scallions and pour 2-3 Tbsp hot oil on top of steamed fish and serve immediately. Use the traditional steaming method for a large whole fish weighing over 1 1/4 lbs as it cooks the fish more evenly than microwaving.

Steamed fish is an Easy, Healthy and Delicious low calorie entrée. **See Photo of Family Dinners,** top left.

Wok Seared Prawns 干煎蝦碌

3/4 -1 lb whole prawns with heads and shell
5 cloves garlic, salt, white pepper, sugar
3 stalks scallions cut into 2 inch lengths
2 Tbsp tapioca starch or 1 Tbsp cornstarch
1 tsp light soy sauce, Oyster sauce
1/2 tsp double deluxe soy sauce (Lee KumKee)
A dash of dark soy sauce for color
2-3 Tbsp oil

Look for fresh, white, firm prawns with translucent shells in Chinese supermarkets that carry lots of fresh seafood. Sprinkle prawns with 1 1/2 tsp salt while deveining (leave the shells and heads on the prawns.) Salt improves the texture of shrimp. Rinse thoroughly in cold water. Drain and pat dry with paper towel. Sprinkle prawns with tapioca starch or cornstarch, salt and pepper.

Heat wok until it's very hot; add oil, swirl oil, and stir-fry prawns with garlic, white pepper and soy sauces. When the prawns are half done (3-4 minutes depending on the range) add scallions. Stir fry another minute until scallions are ready. Season to taste with oyster sauce and a dash of sugar.

The seared prawns have a rich succulent juice encrusted inside the shells. This is another **Easy and Delicious** Seafood Entrée. If you find excellent quality giant prawns, this becomes a **gourmet seafood entrée.** Giant prawns with heads are not readily available in Chinese supermarkets. But medium size prawns with heads can be easily found, and they are prepared the same way as the giant prawns with reduced cooking time. Don't overcook prawns as they cook very quickly.

Crab Roe with Tofu 蟹粉豆腐

1 package Silken Tofu (soft)
1/2 cup shelled crab meat
1 Tbsp crab paste (contains crab roe)
1 Tbsp tapioca starch or 1 1/2 tsp cornstarch
1 Tbsp Shaoxing cooking wine
Dash of Lee Kum Kee double deluxe
soy sauce, optional

2 tsp oyster sauce
1 tsp sesame oil
Salt, pepper
1/2 tsp sugar
1/4 cube chicken bouillon cube
3 cloves garlic, sliced
2 Tbsp oil

Score silken tofu into 1/2 inch x 1/4 inch rectangles. Drain the tofu in a fine flat sieve to get rid of the extra water. While tofu is draining, sprinkle tapioca starch or cornstarch on tofu. Set aside for 10 min. Heat wok on high, and add oil.

Stir-fry tofu with garlic, add crab paste, crabmeat, wine, bouillon softened with 1 Tbsp water, salt, pepper, oyster sauce, sesame oil and sugar to taste. Do not stir too much as the tofu will break apart. This is a favorite Shanghai style dish, rich with crab roe, color, and flavor.   You will love it just as much as my family and friends. **See Photo of Family Dinners,** bottom left. See Photo of ingredients for crab paste on P.17.

This is a 12 minute **Easy and Delicious Gourmet** recipe.

Stuffed Melon with Shrimp 釀節瓜

2 medium size fuzzy melons (looks like a giant zucchini with fine fuzzy hair)
1/4 lb shrimp, shelled and deveined
2 black mushrooms, presoaked 4 hrs or overnight
1 slice white bread, crusts removed
1/2 tsp light soy sauce, white pepper
1/2 tsp Lee Kum Kee double deluxe soy sauce
Oyster sauce and a little sugar
1 1/2 tsp tapioca starch or 1 tsp cornstarch
2 cloves of garlic, sliced
1 cup chicken broth and 1/2 cup mushroom water

Peel the fuzzy melon and cut into 1 inch sections crosswise. Scoop out the seed centers of the melon with a teaspoon or small paring knife. Soak bread center in water; squeeze out excess water.
Discard mushroom stems and mix mushrooms with shrimp, bread center, in a food processor for a few seconds until you have a coarse pâte. Shrimp can be diced and minced using a sharp knife instead of a food processor. Mix pâte with cornstarch, salt, wine, and stuff pâte into melon center.

Grease a large Teflon pan and lightly brown both sides of stuffed melon sections using medium heat. Add chicken broth, mushroom water, garlic, the cored seed centers of the melon, soy sauces mixed with tapioca starch, white pepper and bring everything to a boil. Reduce heat to medium, cover and cook until the stuffed melon is done (30-40 min.) Season to taste with a dash of oyster sauce, double deluxe soy sauce, and sugar. Some may prefer to leave out the cored seed centers of the melon. You could leave the pan cover open to quicken the evaporation of the broth during the last 10 minutes. Garnish with Chinese parsley.

Traditionally the melon is stuffed with minced pork.   Serves 4. **See photo of Family Dinners** in Seafood section.

Shrimp with Soy Beans 毛豆蝦仁

1/2 lb shrimp
2 cups of frozen green soy beans
3-4 cloves garlic
1 Tbsp tapioca starch or cornstarch

1 tsp pale dry sherry or Shaoxing cooking wine
2 Tbsp corn oil or peanut oil
Salt & white pepper, 1 tsp sugar

This is a great dish for busy professionals who have no time to do last minute shopping and want dinner in 10 minutes. Buy frozen uncooked shrimp that is shelled and deveined.

Defrost shrimp and soybeans in the refrigerator ahead of time. Put 1 tsp salt on shrimp while prepping it. Salt improves the texture of shrimp meat. Rinse in cold water, drain, and dry with paper towel. Marinate shrimp with tapioca starch or cornstarch, salt, pepper, and garlic.

Microwave soybeans on serving plate for 1 minute if beans are frozen. Heat wok until it's very hot; add oil, swirl oil and stir-fry shrimp and garlic. Add cooking wine, and toss in the soybeans when shrimp is almost done.   Season to taste with salt and sugar. Voilà, you have an **Easy, Healthy and Delicious** entrée in minutes.

Variation using fresh sugar peas instead of soy beans. Remove tendrils on sugar peas. Wash, spin dry, and microwave for 1 1/2-2 1/2 minutes until sugar peas are almost done and still crunchy. Add to shrimp and stir-fry 1 minute just like the shrimp with soy beans. Season to taste with salt and sugar. It's another **Easy and Delicious** recipe.

Shrimp Stuffed Tofu 蝦釀豆腐

1 package of fried tofu
1/2 lb shrimp, shelled and deveined
2 piece of sliced bread center
(white bread, crust removed)
3 black mushrooms, pre-soaked 4 hrs
2 cups broccoli florets or 1 bunch baby bok
choy, cut into 1 1/2 inch lengths

1 1/2 cup chicken broth
1 tsp Lee Kum Kee double deluxe
soy sauce, oyster sauce
1 tsp cornstarch
1 tsp Shaoxing cooking wine or pale
dry sherry
Salt, pepper, oil

Prep the Shrimp Pâte.
Shell, clean and devein shrimp. While cleaning shrimp, put 1 tsp salt on shrimp to improve the texture. Then rinse off salt in cold water and dry shrimp. Remove stems from mushrooms and cut into quarters. Mix shrimp, mushrooms, and bread in a food processor for 30-60 seconds until you get a coarse pâte texture. Season pâte with salt, pepper, wine, 1/2 tsp cornstarch.

Stuffing and Cooking the Tofu
Cut each piece of tofu into 4 triangles; make a slit on the long side of each triangle, and stuff shrimp pâte into the tofu. Heat 1 Tbsp oil in a Teflon pan. Lightly brown the stuffed tofu with the stuffed shrimp facing down on the pan.

In a saucepan, heat chicken broth with some mushroom water, double deluxe soy sauce, salt, pepper, 1/2 tsp cornstarch, and the wine. Pour over stuffed tofu. Cook on medium for 30-40 minutes. Season to taste with oyster sauce and a little sugar.

Microwave broccoli florets or bok choy for 3-6 minutes until vegetable is tender but not overcooked. Serve stuffed tofu surrounded with vegetables. Pour remaining juice over tofu and green vegetables.

A variation of this recipe is the Shrimp Stuffed Mushrooms.
Stuff 10 presoaked black mushrooms (stems removed) with shrimp pâte. Use the same method as above to cook the mushrooms in a Teflon pan, with the mushrooms on the bottom and the shrimp facing up. Sprinkle minced Virginia ham on the stuffed mushrooms; use the same broth described above to cook on medium for about 30 minutes. Add baby bok choy or broccoli florets surrounding the mushrooms during the last 8 minutes, with the lid off so that the vegetables stay green. The broccoli florets could be microwaved first until almost tender and then combined with the stuffed mushrooms during the last 5 minutes. Serves 4.

Seafood with Steamed Tofu 海鮮蒸豆腐

15 oz package of Silken Tofu (soft tofu)
1/2 lb medium size shrimp, shelled and deveined
1/8 lb bay scallops (optional)
3 dried black mushrooms, presoaked overnight, stems removed, and diced
1/2 cup defrosted frozen peas or soy beans
2 stalks scallions, diced
2 cloves garlic, sliced
1 Tbsp tapioca starch or 1 tsp cornstarch
2 tsp Lee Kum Kee double deluxe soy sauce
Oyster sauce
Salt, white pepper, sugar, 2 Tbsp oil

Prepare shrimp by sprinkling 1 tsp salt on the shrimp while cleaning and prepping it. Salt improves the texture of the shrimp. Cut the shrimp in half. Rinse in cold water and dry with paper towel. Lightly season shrimp and bay scallops with salt, white pepper, and 1 Tbsp tapioca starch or 1 tsp cornstarch. Set aside.

Open the package of silken tofu, and squeeze the sides of the box to loosen the tofu. Invert the tofu into a wide sieve and let it drain for 15 minutes to get rid of excess water. Slice the tofu into half its thickness and spread it onto a serving dish that can be microwaved. Discard excess water which accumulates in the dish. Sprinkle double deluxe soy sauce, oyster sauce, salt, and white pepper on tofu. Microwave on high for 3-5 minutes. Remove excess liquid.

Heat wok until it's very hot. Add oil, swirl oil, and stir-fry shrimp, bay scallops and garlic; add diced mushrooms, peas or soy beans, and scallions while stir-frying. Season to taste with a dash of double deluxe soy sauce, oyster sauce, and sugar. Pour seafood on top of heated tofu. Serve immediately.

Microwaving the tofu is equivalent to steaming it, only it's simpler and faster. This is a very low calorie dish that goes well with rice. It's an **Easy, Healthy and Delicious** entrée that can be prepared in a few minutes if you have presoaked mushrooms.

Shrimp Stuffed Egg Plants 蝦釀矮瓜

1/3 lb shrimp, shelled and deveined
3 Japanese egg plants, sliced diagonally into 1 inch pieces
1 piece of sliced white bread, crusts removed, soaked in water first to soften bread,
then squeeze out extra water
3 black mushrooms, presoaked for 4 hrs or overnight
1-1 1/2 cups of chicken broth
1 1/2 tsp tapioca starch or 1 tsp cornstarch
1 tsp Shaoxing cooking wine or pale sherry
1/2 tsp Lee Kum Kee double deluxe soy sauce
Salt, white pepper, oyster sauce, oil

Buy shelled and deveined shrimp if possible. While cleaning the shrimp, put 2 tsp salt on shrimp to improve its texture. Rinse off salt in cold water and dry with paper towel.
Remove stems from mushrooms and cut into quarters.

Mix shrimp, mushrooms, and bread in a food processor for 30 seconds until you get a coarse pâte. Or you could do it by hand. Season pâté with salt, pepper, cornstarch, and wine.

Cut half way through the one-inch diagonal eggplant pieces. Stuff 1 tsp of pâte into the middle of each egg plant diagonal.

Lightly brown the stuffed egg plant pieces in a Teflon pan with 2 Tbsp oil, putting the shrimp pâte face down on the Teflon pan. Mix 1 cup of chicken broth with salt, pepper, double deluxe soy sauce, tapioca starch, wine, and pour over stuffed eggplants. Using the Teflon pan, cook on medium low for 30 minutes or until the stuffed eggplants are tender. Add mushroom water if necessary. Season to taste with oyster sauce and a dash of double deluxe soy sauce and sugar. Garnish with Chinese parsley. Serves 4.

This dish is traditionally deep fried in oil. Since eggplant soaks up oil like an insatiable sponge, the vegetable is so oily that I break out in pimples if I indulge too much of it. So this recipe uses minimal amount of oil with chicken broth. Just think of the calories saved and the overall health benefits in consuming less oil in our diet. Any extra shrimp pâte could be used for shrimp toast or shrimp stuffed tofu.

Slivered Pressed Tofu with Shrimp 干絲炒蝦仁

4 pieces of pressed tofu, slivered
1/4 lb shrimp, shelled and deveined
2 Tbsp slivered Virginia ham
3 cloves garlic
1 cup defrosted soy beans, optional

1/2 cup slivered bamboo shoots, optional
1 cup chicken broth, 1 Tbsp cooking wine
1 tsp tapioca starch or cornstarch
1/2 tsp Lee Kum Kee double deluxe soy sauce
Salt, white pepper, sugar, 2 Tbsp oil

Buy small, shelled and deveined shrimp to save time in preparation. If small shrimp is not available, cut medium size shrimp to small 1/2 inch pieces. Sprinkle 1 tsp salt on shrimp for a few minutes, then rinse with cold water. Salt improves the texture of shrimp. Dry with paper towel and season shrimp with salt, pepper, and tapioca starch. Set aside.

Sliver white pressed tofu to very fine match stick lengths; make the slivers as thin as possible. Cook slivered tofu and slivered Virginia ham in chicken broth for 5-10 minutes on medium heat.

Heat wok to high; add oil, swirl oil and stir fry shrimp with garlic. Add wine, double deluxe soy sauce, soy beans, and bamboo shoots, a dash of sugar. Season to taste and pour on top of hot slivered press tofu. The appealing part of this delightful dish is the thin slivers of tofu cooked in a savory chicken broth, accented with shrimp or chicken slivers. This is a low calorie **Easy and Delicious** entrée. Serves 4. See **Variation of Slivered Pressed Tofu with Chicken** on p.57.

Beef with Snap Pea Pods

Beef & Pork

Beef with Fresh Green Vegetables
Filet Mignon with Fresh Shitake Mushrooms
Green Beans with Minced Sirloin
Spiced Beef
Braised Pork Shoulder & Bean Curd Knots
Braised Pork with Mustard Cabbage

Beef with Green Vegetables
鮮菜炒牛肉

1/2 lb flank steak, sliced
6 black mushrooms, presoaked 5 hrs
or 1 can whole straw mushrooms
3 cups broccoli florets,
cut to 1" pieces or 3 cups
asparagus tips
1/4 tsp baking soda with
1 Tbsp water
1 tsp pale dry sherry or Shaoxing cooking wine
1 tsp light soy sauce, 1/2 tsp double deluxe soy
sauce (LeeKumKee)
2 tsp tapioca starch or corn starch
Salt and white pepper, sugar
5 cloves fresh garlic, sliced
3 stalks scallions, cut into 2 " lengths
Premium oyster flavored sauce
2 Tbsp corn or peanut oil

Cut asparagus into 1 1/2 inch lengths using
the Roll Cut method. Trim away the fat
and white tendons from the flank steak.
Cut flank steak into 1 1/2 inch length strips.
Then slice flank steak against the grain into
1/8 inch thickness.

Marinate beef in 1/4 tsp baking soda and
1 Tbsp water (baking soda tenderizes the
beef), tapioca starch, soy sauces, wine,
salt, and pepper. Set aside.

Save the water from the dried black
mushrooms, as it adds fragrance to food.
Remove stems and cut black mushrooms
into quarters or sixth triangles. Canned
straw mushrooms should be drained and
left whole if the mushrooms are small,
and cut in halves if large.

Place a piece of wax paper on top of the
plate of broccoli or asparagus so that the
vegetable cooks quickly and evenly.
Microwave broccoli florets or asparagus
tips for 1 1/2 to 3 min until it is 3/4 cooked
and still crunchy.

Heat wok until it's very hot; pour oil in
wok, swirl oil and stir fry garlic and
marinated beef on high.

Toss in all the mushrooms, and continue
to stir fry, adding a little wine or mushroom
water to keep the steam sizzling. Add
scallions. Beef cooks quickly.

When it's almost done, toss in vegetables
and season to taste with oyster sauce and
a little sugar. **Serves 4-6** This is an **Easy,
Healthy and Delicious** entrée.

Variation: **Beef with Spinach** Toss 4-5
cups of uncooked prewashed spinach when
beef is almost cooked. Stir a minute until
leaves are moistened, season to taste and
serve immediately. It's another **Easy,
Healthy and Delicious** entrée.

Filet Mignon with Fresh Shitake Mushrooms
鮮菇炒牛肉

The Filet Mignon with Fresh Shitake Mushrooms will tickle your Epicurean palate.

2 filet mignon steaks (1/2 - 3/4 lb total)
1/4 lb Shitake mushrooms
1/2 lb asparagus tips or 1/2 lb sugar peapods
5 cloves garlic
3 stalks scallions cut into 1 1/2"lengths
2 tsp cornstarch
1 tsp light soy sauce, oyster sauce
salt, white pepper, 3 Tbsp oil, sugar
1 tsp Shaoxing wine or pale dry sherry
2 Tbsp chicken broth

Trim the filet mignon of all fat and white tendons. Slice against the grain into generous 1/8 inch (thicker than 1/8 inch, and just under 1/4 inch) thickness by 1 1/2 inch lengths. Filet mignon does not need any tenderizing, so it only needs to be marinated with soy sauce, cornstarch, wine, salt and white pepper.   Set aside.

Break off tough ends of asparagus and discard. Use roll and cut method: cut diagonally, then roll the spear 1/3 and cut diagonally again until the asparagus spear is cut into 1 " lengths. This method of cutting increases the cooking surface and also gives you a tasty vegetable with a pretty cut. Wash asparagus and microwave on high for 1 1/2 minutes. Asparagus will be barely cooked and crispy. If using sugar peapods, peel off the tendrils on both sides of the pods. Wash and microwave the same way as asparagus. Set aside.

Wash shitake mushrooms and remove stems. Stir-fry mushrooms in 1 Tbsp oil, add wine, 2 Tbsp chicken broth, soy sauce, salt, pepper, and simmer for 5-10 minutes until tender. Add sugar to taste. Shitake mushrooms could be slightly bitter; that's why we cook it separately first, with sugar added.

Heat wok until it's very hot. Pour 3 Tbsp oil in wok, swirl oil and stir-fry on high the beef and garlic until beef is 80% done. Do not overcook. Add whole mushrooms, wine, and asparagus or sugar peapods to beef; continue stir-frying and season with a little oyster sauce to taste. Serve immediately.

This is an **Easy, Healthy and Delicious gourmet** treat. Serves 6 for a Chinese dinner with multiple entrées.

Green Beans & Minced Sirloin 豆角炒牛肉

1/2 lb lean ground sirloin beef
1/2 lb baby green beans, cut into
1/8 inch pieces
8 presoaked black mushrooms, cut into
1/8 inch cubes
1/4 cup winter bamboo shoots, cut into
1/8 inch cubes
5 cloves garlic, minced
1/4 cup dried shrimp, shredded or minced in
food processor

1/4 cup roasted peanuts
1 tsp light soy sauce
1 tsp oyster sauce
1 tsp mushroom seasoning (adds flavor)
Salt, white pepper, sugar
1 Tbsp Shaoxing wine or pale dry sherry
2 Tbsp oil
1 iceberg lettuce, leaves trimmed into scallop
shaped lettuce cups

Trim stem ends of green beans, wash, and cut into 1/8 inch pieces. Microwave 2 minutes. Mince dried shrimp and garlic in food processor for 1-2 minutes, or until shrimp is shredded.

Heat wok until it's very hot. Pour oil in wok, swirl oil and stir fry ground sirloin with shredded shrimp, garlic and wine, breaking the ground beef into tiny pebble like pieces. Add green beans and mushroom, bamboo shoots, and seasoning; stir-fry until beans are done and still crunchy, adding some extra cooking wine or mushroom water if liquid is needed. Since the sirloin is very lean, this dish has very little fat. Season to taste with oyster sauce and some sugar. Sprinkle roasted peanuts on top just before serving so that the peanuts are crunchy. This recipe serves 6.

This dish is usually made with lean ground pork. I modified the recipe to suit contemporary young people who favor beef over pork. By using lean ground sirloin, I can control the fat content of ground beef better than ground pork.

The recipe is nutritionally healthy, colorful and tasty, in addition to being an **Easy, Healthy and Delicious** entrée or appetizer. Serve with iceberg lettuce cups if you are using it as a hot appetizer.

Spiced Beef 五香牛肉

1 large piece of beef shank, whole
5 star anise
1 tsp peppercorn
2 Tbsp dark soy sauce
1 Tbsp light soy sauce
White pepper
1 piece of ginger, peeled

5 cloves garlic
1 Tbsp Shaoxing cooking
wine or pale dry sherry
2 stalks scallions
1 Tbsp raw sugar
Cilantro for garnish

It's best to buy beef shank that is all trimmed and ready for cooking. Place the beef in a pot that is just large enough to hold the meat. Fill the pot with water half way up the beef shank. Bring the water to a boil with the beef and skim off the scum on top as the water boils.

Add all the above ingredients except sugar and bring to a boil before reducing the heat to low. Simmer on low for two hours. During the last half hour if there is a lot of liquid left in the pot, you could leave the pot lid open to facilitate evaporation and reduction of liquid. Turn the range to medium to speed up evaporation until you have about 1 cup of liquid in the pot. Do not walk away from the pot when the lid is off. Watch that the meat does not burn.

Add raw sugar to create a dark shimmering glaze on the beef shank and season to taste. Turn off the heat and let the beef cool. Refrigerate beef shank for a few hours and slice into very thin pieces. It is easier to slice the shank into thin pieces when the beef is cold. Discard star anise and peppercorn. Brush a thin coat of sauce on the sliced beef shank. Arrange sliced shank on a serving plate and garnish with cilantro.

Serve beef shank cold as an appetizer or entrée. Serves 10-12 for a Chinese dinner. In a banquet, the beef shank is often one of 5-8 cold appetizers arranged on a large serving platter served as the first course. Other assortments might include Vegetarian Goose, White Chicken, Sea Jelly Fish, Candied Pecans. Beef shank is a very lean cut of beef.

Braised Pork Shoulder & Knotted Bean Curd Sheet
百頁蹄膀

1 whole pork picnic with bone and skin
8oz package, frozen bean curd knot百頁
(They look like Italian bow-tie pasta)
5 black mushrooms, presoaked overnight
1 cup wood ear mushrooms, presoaked
5 pieces star anise, 5 cloves garlic
5 cups prewashed spinach
3 stalks scallions
2 Tbsp dark soy sauce
1 Tbsp light soy sauce
1 Tbsp LKK double deluxe soy sauce
2 Tbsp soy sauce paste
1 Tbsp Shaoxing wine or pale dry sherry
Lumps of raw sugar (2- 3 Tbsp)

Bring the pork picnic to a boil in a large pot of water for 1-2 minutes; drain and rinse pork in cold water. Rub 1 Tbsp dark soy sauce on the skin and meat and let it stand for 30 minutes so the dark soy sauce colors the skin and meat. Trim mushroom stems and cut into quarters. Clean and trim the ends of wood ear mushrooms. Parboil bean curd knots with 1/8 tsp baking soda and 2 cups of boiling water for 2 minutes. Rinse and drain.

Submerge 3/4 of the pork picnic, skin side up, in a fresh pot of water; add ginger, garlic, scallions, star anise, soy sauces, and wine. Bring to a boil and simmer on low for 1 1/2 hr. Flip over meat with the skin facing down and simmer for 1 1/2 hr. Try to turn the meat without breaking the skin. Pour out sauce and chill in refrigerator to skim off the fat. Put the degreased sauce back in the pot with the braised pork shoulder; add bean curd knots, mushrooms and raw sugar. Bring contents to a boil and simmer 1 1/2 hours. Add more dark soy sauce for color as desired. The meat is sufficiently tender when a chopstick can readily go through it. Leave pot lid open if you want the liquid to evaporate quickly during the last hour leaving 2 cups of rich, dark gravy. Thicken gravy with l Tbsp dissolved tapioca starch in gravy and cook 1 minute. Season to taste.

Prewashed spinach is added the last minute and does not need to be cooked, just coated with gravy. Discard star anise, ginger and scallions. Line the serving plate with bean curd knots, and top with braised pork, mushrooms, and spinach. This is a scrumptious Shanghai style braised pork, rich with flavor and color. Serves 8-10.

Braised Pork with Mustard Cabbage 梅菜扣肉

One slab of whole bacon with skin五花腩
Pickled mustard cabbage leaf, 1 cup, diced 梅菜
4 Tbsp dark soy sauce, 4 Tbsp light soy sauce
1 Tbsp LKK double deluxe soy sauce
1Tbsp Shaoxing wine or pale dry sherry
5 cloves of garlic
3 Tbsp oil, Salt, white pepper, sugar

At a Chinese market, select a lean slab of whole bacon. Cut into 2 portions.
For each portion, rub 1 Tbsp dark soy sauce over the whole bacon. Let it stand for 30 min. On medium, brown the two pieces of whole bacon on all sides until lightly brown. Put a splatter screen over the bacon while browning.

Slice the bacon against the grain into 1/4 inch thick pieces.
Marinade: For each of the two portions, mix 1 Tbsp dark soy sauce, 2 Tbsp light soy sauce, 1 Tbsp double deluxe soy sauce, and 1 Tbsp sugar and coat sliced bacon with the marinade.

Arrange the sliced, dipped bacon in a dish, with the skin of the bacon facing down, and the slices lying slanted and leaning against the other cut pieces in the exact order as they were cut.

Use the remainder of the marinade to sauté the garlic with the pickled vegetables; add wine. Make more marinade if you don't have enough. Repeat the same procedure for the second portion of the bacon in a separate dish so that you will have a double portion for the steaming.

Spread the seasoned pickled vegetables evenly on the bacon slices. Cover with wax paper, then plastic wrap, and steam 4 hrs. The dish sits on a rack inside a large pot with 2-3 inches of boiling water. Add boiling water periodically to make sure there is sufficient water in the pot. When ready to serve, place a larger dish over the braised pork, then invert the dish over a sink in case the juice spills a little. Garnish with Chinese parsley.

I generally make the second portion at the same time so that the meat can be steamed simultaneously. This is my husband's favorite dish, which I serve only occasionally because of the fat in the skin. He insists on eating the skin, which he considers irresistible. So to avoid an argument over cholesterol matters, I freeze the second portion and serve it when he really has the urge for this rich dish. I enjoy the lean meat.

Empress Chicken

Poultry

♥ Chicken with Pressed Tofu, Mushrooms
豆腐干炒雞絲

1 chicken breast filet
2 pieces of white pressed tofu
5 black mushrooms, presoaked for 4 hrs
1/2 green bell pepper, 1/2 red bell pepper
1/2 can of straw mushrooms, optional
3 cloves of minced garlic
1 1/2 tsp cornstarch
1 tsp Shaoxing cooking wine or
pale dry sherry
Salt, white pepper, oyster sauce, 2 Tbsp oil

It is easier to slice chicken breast when it is half frozen. Slice to thin 1/8 inch thickness, then cut against the grain into thin slivers, match stick size.
Marinate chicken breast with cornstarch, salt, pepper, and wine. Set aside. Cut pressed tofu, mushrooms, and bell peppers into match stick size.

Heat wok until it's very hot. Pour oil in wok, swirl oil and stir fry on high the slivered chicken and minced garlic. Add mushrooms and slivered tofu while stir frying. Add slivered bell peppers last, just before seasoning the food to taste with a little oyster sauce and sugar. Serves 4.

This is a versatile chicken entrée that has infinite variations made by adding or substituting vegetables at your discretion. This is an **Easy, Healthy and Delicious** entrée.

Variation 1: Chicken with Mushrooms and Bean Sprouts (Vietnamese Spring Rolls)
If you are making a larger quantity with plans to set aside part of the dish for Spring Rolls, then you would prepare the chicken in the same way and use parboiled bean sprouts in place of bell peppers and pressed tofu. The bean sprouts are parboiled in a large pot of water. Drain water thoroughly and toss sprouts into the wok with the cooked chicken and season to taste. Instead of parboiling, bean sprouts can also be stir fried with no oil in a hot dry wok for a few minutes to get rid of excess water. The sprouts should be still crunchy. Set aside. Combine bean sprouts in the last minute with the sautéed hot chicken ingredients and season to taste.

Variation 2: Chicken with Salted Mustard Greens and Soy Beans雪菜毛豆炒雞絲
Cut and sliver the chicken and stir-fry the same way with sliced black mushrooms, 1/2 cup of salted mustard greens (咸菜), 1 cup of frozen green soy beans, and 2 pieces of slivered pressed tofu. This can be a main dish and also makes a great topping over soup noodles for lunch. Traditionally this dish is made with lean pork rather than chicken. In recent years, I am using more chicken than pork, and find it just as good.

Note: The Chicken filet on this page shows the meat slivered. The chicken is sliced into thin 1 1/2 inch pieces on p. 57, and diced on p. 58 with different presentations and taste.

♥ Curry Chicken 咖哩雞

3 chicken drumsticks & thighs
1 red yam, 1 potato, peeled
3 cups baby carrots
1 onion, cut into 1 inch pieces
1/2 cup roasted peanuts
Mango chutney or mango salsa
6 cloves of garlic, minced
2 tsp curry powder
1 cup coconut milk or chicken broth
Salt, pepper, sugar, 2 Tbsp oil
2 Tbsp pale dry sherry or Shaoxing wine
Steamed rice, Cilantro for garnish

Ask the butcher to chop the drumsticks and thighs into 1 inch pieces with bones. Remove skin (optional) and fat from chicken; rinse and dry with paper towel. Cut peeled potato in half, then use the roll cut method to cut potato and yam into serving pieces.

See section on Cutting Methods in Cooking Tips. Start rice in rice cooker.

Heat wok until it's very hot; pour oil in wok, swirl oil and stir fry minced garlic, onions and chicken first; add salt, pepper, curry powder, a little at a time, and stir fry for 5-10 minutes on high. Add onions, carrots, yam, potato, wine, and coconut milk or chicken broth, tossing constantly for 5 minutes on high; then cover wok and cook on low (20-30) minutes, turning the ingredients a few times until chicken and vegetables are very tender. Ranges vary so the cooking time will also. Season to taste with a little sugar. Add more curry if you want a stronger curry flavor. Serve curry chicken over rice with mango chutney or mango salsa and crunchy peanuts in small separate side dishes. Garnish with cilantro. **Serves 4-6.**

Curry Chicken is an **Easy, Healthy and Delicious** Chinese entrée that came via India.

56

♥ Chicken with Mushrooms 冬菇炒雞片

1/2 chicken breast, sliced
6 black mushrooms, presoaked for 4 hrs or overnight, and sliced into 1 1/2 inch pieces
l handful of cloud ear mushrooms (optional) presoaked, rinsed, and sliced
3-4 cups sugar peapods with tendrils removed
1/4 cup sliced winter bamboo shoots (optional)
3 cloves garlic, 2 stalks scallions cut into 1 1/2 inches
1/4 tsp baking soda, 1 1/2 tsp tapioca starch or cornstarch
1 tsp Shaoxing cooking wine or pale dry sherry
Salt and white pepper
Oyster sauce, 2 Tbsp oil

For easy cutting, slice chicken breast when it is half frozen. Slice to 1/8 inch thickness, then cut the slices against the grain into 1 inch x 1 1/2 inch.
Marinate chicken breast in baking soda mixed with 1 Tbsp water, tapioca starch, soy sauce, salt, pepper, and wine. Set aside.
Remove mushroom stems; cut mushrooms into quarters or sixths. See section on **Dry Ingredients and Mushrooms** to save time in preparation.

Microwave sugar pea pods for 1 1/2 minutes. Check to see if pea pods are almost done. They may need another minute in the microwave as microwaves vary and may require more or less time. We want the pea pods still crunchy.
Heat wok until it's very hot. Pour oil in wok, swirl oil and stir fry on high the sliced chicken and garlic. Add mushrooms, sugar peapods, bamboo shoots (optional) and scallions while stir frying. Season to taste with a little oyster sauce and sugar. Serves 4.

This is an **Easy, Healthy, and Delicious** stir-fry dish that can be made in a few minutes if all the ingredients are ready.

Variation: Slivered Press Tofu with Chicken 干絲炒雞片

Slivered Pressed Tofu with Chicken is a double variation of the **Chicken with Mushrooms** and the Slivered Pressed Tofu with Shrimp on p. 46.
Prepare sliced chicken breast filet the same way marinated with garlic, baking soda, tapioca starch, and wine. Slice black mushrooms, bamboo shoots, the same way as the chicken recipe. Sliver 2 pieces of white pressed tofu to very fine match stick lengths; make the slivers as thin as possible. Slice 6 stalks of scallions to 1 1/2 inch lengths.   See photo of pressed tofu in Fresh and Dry Chinese Ingredients, p.17.

Stir-fry the chicken slices in hot oil the same way and add slivered pressed tofu to chicken when chicken is almost ready. Add 1/2 cup of chicken broth to the mixture while stir-frying. Add cut scallions, toss and season to taste with oyster sauce and a dash of sugar.   It's another **Easy, Healthy and Delicious** entrée that is a family favorite. It is a very substantial dish with the slivered tofu cooked in a savory sauce.

♥ Diced Chicken with Corn, Mushrooms, and Pine Nuts
松子炒雞丁

1 whole chicken breast filet
5 presoaked dried mushrooms, cut into 1/3 inch cubes
1 small handful roasted pine nuts
1/2 -1 cup fresh, frozen, or canned whole corn kernels
1/4 tsp baking soda
4-5 cloves fresh crushed garlic, crushed
3 stalks scallions, diced
1-2 tsp cornstarch depending on the amount of chicken
1 tsp oyster sauce
Salt & white pepper
1 tsp pale dry sherry or Shaoxing cooking wine
2 Tbsp oil

For ease of handling, cut chicken breast into 1/3- inch cubes when it's half frozen. Marinate chicken with baking soda, 1 Tbsp water and the wine, garlic, cornstarch, salt, and white pepper. Set aside. Heat wok until it's very hot; add oil and swirl oil in wok. Stir-fry chicken and diced mushrooms with garlic; add a little wine or chicken broth while stir frying to keep it sizzling. Add corn, scallions, and season to taste with salt, oyster sauce, and sugar. Sprinkle pine nuts and serve immediately. Do not overcook chicken. Depending on the amount of chicken used, the amounts of corn and pine nuts are adjusted to balance the meat.

The Diced Chicken with Corn, Mushrooms, and Pine Nuts is an **Easy, Healthy and Delicious** entrée or hot appetizer served with lettuce cups. Serves 4-6

♥ "Rich and Famous" Chicken 富貴雞

There is a charming story that goes with the name of this chicken, which is actually Beggar's Chicken.
A hungry beggar stole a live chicken from a farmer. In order to hide the chicken and protect himself from being caught, he buried the live chicken in mud.
Lacking any cooking utensils, he improvised a clever solution by roasting the chicken, encrusted in mud, over an open fire, and enjoyed a deliciously fragrant meal.

1 whole chicken
5 Tbsp light soy sauce
1 Tbsp dark soy sauce
1 Tbsp oyster sauce
Salt, white pepper

1 Tbsp Shaoxing cooking wine
6 cloves garlic
2 stalks scallions cut into 2" lengths
2 star anise

The restaurants serve this chicken with pomp and style. The waiter serves the chicken covered with a terracotta shaped rooster. Since Chinese people are often superstitious, the restaurants changed the name Beggar's Chicken to Rich and Famous Chicken so that people are more likely to order the dish.

Rinse chicken in cold water and dry with paper towel. Mix above ingredients and rub marinade on chicken skin and cavity. Turn over chicken a few times while marinating the bird for 48 hour in the refrigerator.

Wrap and seal marinated chicken with sauce and star anise in two layers of heavy foil. Put chicken in a dish and steam for 2 hours in a covered pot, making sure there is plenty of water. Chicken comes out tender and moist. Chicken can be wrapped in foil and also baked in 375 degrees preheated oven for one hour.

Variation 1 Chicken can also be stuffed with 1 cup stir-fried sliced pork with 1/2 cup sliced mushrooms, 2 Tbsp sliced bamboo shoots, salted turnips, and scallions. Stuffed chicken needs to be steamed or baked 40 minutes longer.
Variation 2 For company, Cornish game hen can be used for individual portions.

My sister Elizabeth gave me this recipe. She sometimes makes it with a vegetarian or cooked noodle stuffing without the meat.

♥ Empress Chicken 貴妃雞

8 chicken drumsticks
6 dried black mushrooms, presoaked 4 hrs or overnight, water saved
1/2 cup dried cloud ear mushrooms, presoaked
1 cup baby carrots
1 large yellow onion, cut into 1" pieces
10 ozs of pre-roasted, shelled, peeled chestnuts, optional (ready to eat)
1/2 cup sliced bamboo shoots

1/2 cup fresh lotus seeds, optional
2 ozs mung bean vermicelli, presoaked
5 cloves garlic, sliced, 2 star anise
2 Tbsp oil, salt, white pepper
1 Tbsp light soy sauce
1 tsp dark soy sauce
1 piece of raw sugar 冰糖
or 1 Tbsp sugar
1 Tbsp Shaoxing cooking wine or sherry
1 cup mushroom water or water

The beauty of this delicious chicken is that the ingredients are all tossed together in the wok, seasoned, and then baked in a covered casserole dish for 40-50 minutes. So it is well worth the effort to presoak some mushrooms and enjoy a robust and fragrant chicken with chestnuts that melt in your mouth.

Soak mushrooms in water. Use water from black mushrooms for cooking later. Discard stems from black mushrooms and cut mushrooms into quarters. Change and discard the water soaking the cloud ear mushrooms until it is clear; trim the hard stem ends of the cloud ear mushrooms. Discard skin from chicken drumsticks (optional) and chop drumsticks in half with cleaver. Rinse in water. Dry with paper towel. Drumsticks could be left whole if you so desire.

Heat wok until it's very hot; pour oil in wok, swirl oil and stir fry garlic and chopped chicken on high. Season with soy sauces and white pepper while stir-frying. Add chestnuts, mushrooms, carrots, wine, star anise, 1 cup mushroom water (from soaking the black mushrooms) and raw sugar. Stir fry and mix the on medium until the raw sugar melts. Add vermicelli, bamboo shoots, and lotus seeds. Bake in a covered casserole in a preheated oven @ 325 degrees for 40-50 minutes. Discard star anise. Instead of baking this dish, you can simmer the chicken on low for 20 minutes after all the ingredients have been added, keeping the wok covered and turning the meats and vegetables in the wok.

You can find the shelled, peeled and ready to eat chestnuts in large Chinese supermarkets. If you cannot buy the ready to eat ones, buy frozen or dried chestnuts and cook them first in chicken broth until tender. The Empress Chicken is traditionally made without chestnuts; I added them because of their distinctive flavor. See photo on chapter page.

♥ White Chicken 白切雞

1 whole chicken or 8-10 drumsticks
10-16 cups chicken broth, depending on the
amount of chicken
2 Tbsp Shaoxing wine or pale dry sherry
2 stalks scallions, slivered in 1 1/2 inch pieces
6 cloves garlic, crushed, salt, white pepper
1 whole piece of ginger, 1 1/2 inches, sliced half
way through

To clean chicken, rub it with salt using
a piece of ginger. Rinse chicken; sprinkle
with salt, white pepper, garlic and
scallions and marinate overnight, covered,
in refrigerator.

Use a large pot with plenty of broth so that
the chicken can be entirely submerged in
the boiling broth. 14-16 cups would entirely
submerge a whole chicken, 10-12 cups
for drumsticks. If you are using a whole
chicken, pull the chicken thighs and
drumsticks away from the body to break the
joints so that the chicken cooks quickly and
more evenly.

Bring the broth to a boil with the scallions,
garlic, ginger and wine. Put whole chicken
or drumsticks in the boiling broth and bring
it to a boil again using medium heat. Cover
and simmer for 15 minutes. Turn off the
range and **Do Not Lift the Cover.** The
residual heat is used to cook the chicken.
After the pot cools completely, take out the
chicken, drain liquid, and cut chicken into
serving pieces. Serves 4-8.
The broth could be used for soup. It's
the same broth used for the Crab Tsiu
Chou Style.

The meat will be very tender and juicy.
Traditionally, a whole chicken is used, but
for the convenience of making dinner for
a small family, you could use drumsticks.

A variation to the White Chicken is to pour
2 Tbsp of hot oil over 3 stalks of slivered
scallions, (cut lengthwise into 1 1/2 inch
lengths) spread on top of the cooked, cut
chicken in the serving plate. The hot oil
and scalded scallions add a distinct
fragrance and taste.

♥ Barbecue Chicken 焗雞

This is a good barbecue for city folks who don't want to be bothered with lighter fluid and charcoal.

8-10 chicken drumsticks or thighs	1 Tbsp cooking wine
6 cloves garlic, crushed	1 1/2 Tbsp honey
2 stalks scallions, chopped fine	Salt and white pepper
1 Tbsp light soy sauce, 1 tsp dark soy sauce	

Wash meat and dry with paper towel. Cut slits across the widest part of the drumsticks and thighs to let marinade penetrate the meat. Slicing the meat cooks it faster and more evenly in the oven. Make a marinade of the soy sauces, wine, honey, and salt and pepper; mix with garlic and scallions and pour over chicken. Mix well. Refrigerate several hours or best overnight. The meat will be tastier when the marinade soaks in overnight.

Line broiler pan with heavy foil. Broil chicken on low (5 inches from the top of the broiler) with the sauce, scallions and garlic; turn the chicken once when it is brown and lightly charred, as in a real barbecue. Watch the broiler by leaving the oven door ajar. To create the desired color of barbecue, you could turn the broiler on high for a short period, watching the chicken carefully so that it does not get too charred.

The Barbecue Chicken is **Easy, Healthy and Delicious** without having to clean the grill.

♥ Tea Smoked Chicken 茶葉煙雞

1 whole chicken	5 cloves garlic, crushed
2 star anise, 2 tsp peppercorns	2 bags of tea (not herbal or green tea)
2 tsp salt, white pepper	2 Tbsp brown sugar, heavy aluminum foil

Wash and clean the skin and cavity of a whole chicken. Dry with paper towel.
Crush star anise and peppercorns. In a dry wok, stir fry the spices with 2 tsp salt on medium heat for 5 minutes. Rub the chicken skin and cavity with garlic and the dry salted spices. Steam the chicken for 1 hour in a covered dish. Drain liquid. Remove the large pieces of spice from the skin and cavity; let the chicken cool.

Line the wok or a roaster with foil. Open 2 bags of tea (any brand of black tea) and mix with 2 Tbsp brown sugar. Place whole chicken on a rack, with the tea and brown sugar on the aluminum foil underneath the rack. Seal the entire wok or roaster with foil.
Place wok over high burner for 10 min. Don't open the cover of the wok or roaster inside the house. Take the entire wok or roaster outside. Place chicken on a serving platter and serve hot or cold. The bird will have the taste and aroma of smoked chicken.

♥ Portuguese Chicken 葡國雞

Portuguese Chicken is a regular Chinese dish that was introduced by the Portuguese who lived in China and Macao. Some of the settlers spoke fluent Chinese. There were many other Europeans including French, English and Russians who lived in Shanghai, spoke Shanghainese and loved Chinese food. I understand there is a group of Russians from Shanghai, now living in New York City who celebrate Chinese New Year, and still speak Shanghainese. As a child, I remember enjoying Russian Soup (羅宋湯) which is basically a beef and vegetable soup with lots of fresh tomatoes. So the Chinese assimilated some of the Western influences by having dishes named after the country of origin. I doubt if we would actually find Portuguese Chicken in Portugal and Russian Soup in Russia.

3 chicken drumsticks & thighs
3 cups baby carrots, cilantro for garnish
2 red yams, 1 potato, peeled
1 onion, cut into 1 inch pieces
6 cloves garlic, minced
2 hard boiled eggs, sliced

1 cup coconut milk, 1/2 cup whole milk
1 1/2 cups chicken broth
Salt, pepper, sugar, 2 Tbsp oil
2 Tbsp pale dry sherry or Shaoxing wine
Steamed rice

Ask the butcher to chop the drumsticks and thighs into 1 inch pieces with bones; or you could use a cleaver to chop the chicken. If you don't want to chop the chicken, then use drumsticks and wing drumsticks. It does save time in preparation. Remove skin (optional) and fat from chicken; rinse and dry with paper towel. Cut peeled potato into quarters, lengthwise, then use the roll cut method to cut potato and yam into serving pieces. See section on Cutting Methods in Cooking Tips.

Heat wok until it's very hot; pour oil in wok, swirl oil and stir fry minced garlic, onions and chicken first; add salt, pepper and stir fry for 5 minutes on high. Add carrots, yams, potato, wine, coconut and regular milk, tossing constantly for 5 minutes on high. Add chicken broth and cook on high for 5 minutes; then cook on low covered (20-30) minutes until chicken and vegetables are tender. Add eggs. Season to taste. Serve with rice.

Coconut milk adds a nice fragrance and taste to the creamy chicken, but chicken broth can be substituted if cholesterol is a matter of concern. Chicken skin and egg yolks can also be deleted. Yam is not part of the traditional ingredients; I added yam for its nutritional value since it's rich in Vitamin A, C, Folate, and Potassium.
Portuguese Chicken is an **Easy, Healthy and Delicious** entrée.

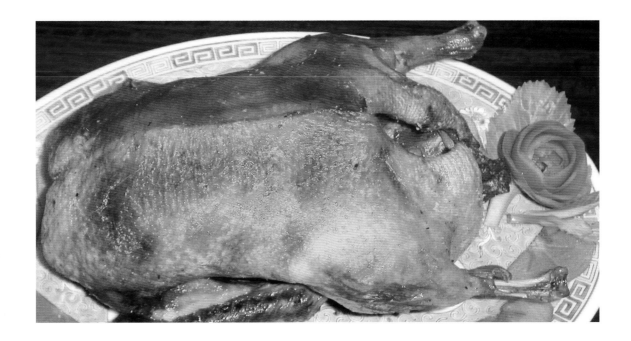

Fragrant Roast Duck 香酥鴨

1 large duck, fresh or frozen
5 cloves garlic
2 stalks scallions, cut to 1 1/2 inches
2 tsp salt, white pepper

1 tsp peppercorns, crushed
2 star anise, crushed
1 Tbsp Shaoxing wine or pale dry sherry

Clean and wipe dry the skin and cavity of the duck. Cut off the tail and fat.
In a dry wok, stir fry salt and peppercorns on low for 5 minutes to let the peppercorn penetrate the salt. Use the side of the cleaver to crush the garlic, mix with salt, peppercorns, and star anise and rub the duck cavity and skin without breaking the skin. Let it stand a few hrs or overnight. Steam the duck for 1 hr. Drain the liquid, and remove the spices without breaking the skin. Set aside.

Time the roasting an hour before dinner time.
Roast the duck in a foil lined pan at 375 degrees for one hour until golden brown. The duck will have most of the fat drained first at the steaming and again in the oven. You can turn off the oven when it looks done. The skin is crispy but not burnt, while the aroma of the fragrant duck is very tantalizing.
This twice degreased **Gourmet** duck should be served hot from the oven.

Braised Duck with Chestnuts P. 66

Braised Duck with Chestnuts 栗子鴨

1 large duck (fresh or frozen)
1 cup dried black cloud mushroom, presoaked and cleaned
8 dried black mushrooms, presoaked
10 ozs frozen shelled chestnuts (or shelled & peeled roasted chestnuts)
5 cloves garlic, 1small piece ginger

2 stalks fresh green onions
5 star anise
1 tsp dark soy sauce
3 Tbsp light soy sauce
1 Tbsp LKK double deluxe soy sauce
Shaoxing cooking wine or pale dry sherry
1/4 cup rock sugar

See section on Dry Ingredients and Mushrooms to save time. Soak 1 cup black cloud mushroom in water. Change and discard water several times until water is clear. Remove hard stem ends of black cloud mushrooms. Set aside. Soak 8 dried black mushrooms in water (save the water for simmering the duck as it adds fragrance to the duck.) Remove stems of mushrooms.

Wash duck and dry with paper towel. Rub 1 tsp dark soy sauce on the skin of the duck. Roast in 400 degree preheated oven for 30 min to degrease duck. Place duck breast side down in a Teflon coated pot. Add reserved mushroom water and enough water to cover over 1/2 of the body of the duck. Add soy sauces, cooking wine, ginger, garlic, scallions, and 4 star anise (put spice in a small pouch that can be discarded when duck is done.)

Bring duck to a boil and cook on low for 2 hrs. The liquid will be reduced to a smaller quantity. Carefully turn over the duck without breaking the skin and continue cooking on low for about an hour until the duck is almost done. Remove all the juice and allow remaining fat to rise; discard the fat. If you ice the juice, the oil separates faster. The second degreasing is crucial because the duck is leaner.

Cook tops differ requiring different cooking time. If the duck looks almost done, then cook the mushrooms, chestnuts, and raw sugar in degreased juice in a separate pot for about 45 minutes before combining with cooked duck. Leave lid open to reduce juice to 4 cups. If the duck needs more time, then cook chestnuts and mushrooms with duck and degreased juice for about 45 minutes. Put some of the cloud ear mushrooms in the duck cavity while simmering. Add dark soy sauce as needed to achieve color.

The pre-roasted, ready to eat chestnuts require minimum cooking. Stir occasionally and baste duck without breaking the duck skin and chestnuts. Discard star anise, ginger, garlic and scallions. Mix 2 Tbsp tapioca starch with 4Tbsp duck gravy and stir into the gravy and cook for a minute. Baste the duck with juice during the last 5 minutes to get a shimmering glaze on the duck skin. Season to taste. Serves 6-10

Enjoy a scrumptious **Gourmet** braised duck that has been twice degreased. The duck meat and chestnuts should melt in your mouth when simmered to perfection. Garnish with Chinese parsley. See Photo.

Bean Curd Knots with Soy Beans

Vegetables

♥ Fresh Mushroom Vegetarian Serenade 鮮菇蛋白素燴

3/4 lb fresh shitake mushrooms
1/4 lb fresh oyster mushrooms
6 egg whites, 3/4 cup chicken broth
2 cloves garlic, sliced

1 1/2 Tbsp oil
1 tsp tapioca starch or 1 tsp cornstarch
Salt, white pepper
Oyster sauce, 1 Tbsp sugar

Prepare garnish with turnip flowers, bok choy heart flowers or broccoli florets. Trim broccoli florets or the 1 1/2 inch bok choy heart with flowers from several bunches of bok choy. Dip in chicken broth and microwave 1-2 minutes.

Beat the egg whites. Stir in chicken broth, and a sprinkling of salt.   Microwave egg whites in a 10 1/2-inch diameter x 1 1/2 inch deep round dish for approximately 3-4 minutes until egg whites are firm.

Wash mushrooms, and remove stems from shitake mushrooms. Save stems for other dishes. Cut large oyster mushrooms into quarters, and leave small ones whole; leave shitake mushrooms whole.

Heat wok until it's very hot. Pour oil in wok, swirl oil and stir fry mushrooms with sliced garlic in oil for a few minutes. Add 1/2 cup of chicken broth, mixed with a little cornstarch, and season to taste with salt, white pepper, a dash of oyster sauce, and 1-2 Tbsp sugar. Continue stir-frying for 2 minutes. Pour fresh mushrooms on top of the hot steamed egg whites. Garnish with turnip flowers, or bok choy heart flowers, or broccoli florets surrounding the mushrooms. Serves 6. **See Garnish & photo** on p 10-11.

This is a beautiful, nutritious, and tasty vegetarian dish. **It's a healthy gourmet** dish for company or family dinners. The white turnips with green pea sprout centers make an impressive and beautiful garnish, but you could enjoy the dish with bok choy heart flowers or broccoli florets, which take less effort instead of the elegant turnip flowers.

♥ Bean Curd Knots with Soy Beans and Mustard Greens
咸菜百頁毛豆

1 8-oz package of frozen bean curd sheets or frozen bean curd knots 百頁
4 ozs fresh frozen soy beans (or 1 1/2 cups)
3/4 cup fresh salted mustard greens (diced and cooked, in refrigerated section)
2 cups chicken broth
1/8 tsp baking soda
1/4 tsp tapioca starch or corn starch
1 Tbsp oil, optional
Sugar

If bean curd sheets are used, first slice the sheets into 1/8 inch widths, then follow the same cooking method.
Cook sliced bean curd sheets or bean curd knots with 1/8 tsp of baking soda in 2 cups of boiling water until the bean curd sheets or knots are soft (about 1-2 minutes in boiling water.) The frozen bean curd knots are tenderized with baking soda. Drain and rinse in cold water. If you buy the refrigerated white bean curd knots (rather than the frozen variety,) then don't parboil with baking soda since the texture is already very soft. I prefer the frozen bean curd knots or frozen sliced bean curd sheets because they don't fall apart after simmering.

Cook softened bean curd sheets or knots in 2 cups of chicken broth for 30-45 minutes. Stir fry soy beans and mustard greens in 1 Tbsp oil on medium heat; add cooked bean curd knots and season to taste with a sprinkle of sugar. Mix 2 tsp tapioca starch with 2 Tbsp broth and whisk into the remaining juice to thicken the juice. For the calorie counters, you can skip the stir frying and just add soy beans and mustard greens to the bean curd knots or sliced bean curd sheets and season to taste with a sprinkle of sugar.

This is one of my favorite **Easy, Healthy, and Delicious** vegetarian dishes that is chock full of vitamin A, calcium, copper, and potassium. **See Photo on P. 67.**

♥ *Abalone King Mushrooms and Mustard Greens*
鮑魚靈芝菇扒菜膽

1 large king mushroom
1 large bunch of mustard greens
2 cups chicken broth
1 tsp oyster sauce or LKK
vegetarian stir-fry sauce, optional
Sauce from 1can of Top Shellfish
from Mexico (optional)
1 tsp vegetable oil
1 tsp tapioca starch or cornstarch
mixed with 2 Tbsp broth
1/4 tsp baking soda
1/2 tsp sugar

This is a dish that we discovered while visiting Sydney, Australia. I noticed a platter of sliced abalone on mustard greens that looked so good that I asked the waiter why that plate of abalone was so white compared to our serving. I was delighted to find out that it was not abalone, but mushrooms. We became addicted to the dish because it not only looked like sliced abalone, but it also tasted like a delicate seafood. It has a delicious meaty texture.

Fresh king mushrooms are not readily available in supermarkets. Try the Chinese grocery stores, which carry this mushroom sometimes. I was not aware of the existence of king mushrooms until after I was introduced to them in Sydney.

Wash and cut fresh mustard greens into long 5-inch pieces. Parboil mustard greens in a large pot of boiling water, lid open, with 1/8 tsp of baking soda until the vegetable is tender (about a minute.) Drain and set aside.

Use a sharp knife to cut mushrooms lengthwise into 1/4 inch slices. Parboil sliced mushrooms in water and 1/4-1/2 tsp baking soda to tenderize the mushrooms. Drain water and rinse mushroom before cooking in chicken broth, on medium for 20-45 minutes, depending on the size of mushrooms.

Heat oil in wok and stir-fry mustard greens with 1/2 cup of juice from mushrooms; add sugar and half of tapioca starch mixture and cook 1/2 minute. Place vegetables on serving plate. Add remaining tapioca starch to hot mushrooms; cook 1/2 minute and season to taste with vegetarian stir-fry sauce. Top mustard greens with sliced king mushrooms.

This is a vegetarian dish that will surprise and delight your relatives and friends.
Make sure you use a good chicken broth as a base for this **Easy, Healthy and Delicious** entrée. Sometimes I cheat by using the sauce from the canned Top Shellfish instead of chicken broth to cook the king mushrooms because the sauce is more tasty than chicken broth. The meat from the Top Shellfish is sliced and served as an appetizer or side dish or used as a noodle topping.

♥ Six Jeweled Vegetables 素六寶

3 pieces of pressed tofu, diced into 1/8 inch cubes
1/2 green pepper, finely chopped
1/2 red pepper, finely chopped
1/4 lb green beans, cut to 1/8 inch pieces, washed and microwave 2 minutes
5 black mushrooms, presoaked 4 hrs or overnight, cut into 1/8 inch pieces
1/4 cup small dried shrimp, mixed in the food processor for 2 minutes until shredded.
1 cup corn, fresh or canned whole kernels
1/4 cup roasted peanuts, shelled (optional)
5 cloves garlic, diced or mixed in food processor with dried shrimp.
1 tsp light soy sauce
1 tsp oyster sauce
Chicken broth
1 tsp mushroom seasoning
Salt, white pepper, a little sugar
1 Tbsp Shaoxing wine or pale dry sherry
2 Tbsp oil

1 head of iceberg lettuce (optional)

Trim iceberg lettuce to 5 inch scallop-shaped cups. (Save lettuce trimming for salad.)
Trim stem ends of baby green beans, wash, cut, and microwave 2 minutes. Set aside.
Heat wok until it's very hot; add 2 Tbsp oil, swirl oil, and stir-fry tofu, black mushrooms, shredded dried shrimp, garlic, and microwave green beans, until beans are ready. Add green and red peppers and corn. Add some chicken broth and some mushroom seasoning so that the ingredients are moist while stir frying, but there should be no extra sauce. Season to taste with salt, pepper, wine, soy sauce, oyster sauce, and a little sugar. Sprinkle a few peanuts on top of the vegetables just before serving so that the nuts are still crunchy.   Serves 6

This makes a very fast and colorful dish, rich with vitamins, minerals, and fiber. It could be served as a main dish or with lettuce leaves for wrapping as a hot appetizer. This vegetarian jewel appeals to the health-conscious and is made with my daughter, Stephanie, in mind. This is an **Easy and Delicious Vegetarian** entrée.

♥ Spinach, Egg White, & Mushroom Medley
菠菜蛋白炒冬菇

6 dried black mushrooms, presoaked 4 hrs or overnight
1 cup cloud ear mushrooms, presoaked and cleaned
5 cups fresh spinach, pre-washed
1/2 cup lotus seeds, cooked, vacuum packed, found in refrigerated section
1/4 cup sliced winter bamboo shoots (optional)
1/2 cup baby corn (optional)
1/2 cup canned fried gluten with mushroom and peanuts
4 egg whites, beaten
1/2 cup chicken broth
2 Tbsp oil
Oyster sauce
Salt, white pepper
1-2 Tbsp sugar

Discard stems from black ear mushrooms, and cut mushrooms into quarters.
Presoak cloud ear mushrooms and change the water used to soak the mushrooms until the water is clear. Discard the water used to soak this mushroom. Discard the black, hard stem ends and cut mushrooms into 1/2 inch pieces.

Beat egg whites in a 2" deep x 5" microwave safe dish. Mix in 1/2 cup of chicken broth and a sprinkling of salt. Microwave 3-4 minutes in serving dish until egg whites are firm. Set aside.

Heat wok until it's very hot. Pour oil in wok, swirl oil and stir-fry black mushrooms. Add cloud ear mushrooms and all ingredients except spinach. Add a little mushroom water or chicken broth, salt, white pepper and oyster sauce. Cook on medium for 5-6 minutes. Add spinach and toss a few times until spinach is moistened and barely cooked. Add sugar and season to taste.

Serve hot vegetarian mix over steamed or microwaved egg whites. Enjoy a colorful and nutritious vegetarian dish that can be whipped up in 5 minutes if the dry ingredients are presoaked. Check the section on Dry Ingredients for preparing mushrooms to save time. Serves 2-4 for a Chinese dinner with multiple entrées.

♥ Winter Melon Vegetarian Gourmet 鼎湖上素

This is a delicious vegetarian dish that is easily tossed together in the wok. The winter melon is cooked separately in chicken broth and is the center piece surrounded by a tasty vegetarian medley. You will love it as much as my family and friends.

1 large section of Winter Melon (about 2 lbs)
6 dried black mushrooms, presoaked for 4 hrs
or overnight
1/2 cup canned straw mushrooms, drained
1/4 cup cloud ear mushrooms, presoaked at least overnight and cleaned
1 can of fried gluten with mushrooms and peanuts (key ingredient)
1/2 cup lotus seeds or gingko nut found in refrigerated section (optional)
1 bundle of mung bean vermicelli (looks like transparent noodles)
1 piece of winter bamboo shoot, sliced (optional ingredient)
1/2 cup of canned baby corn, cut to 1" lengths (optional ingredient)
1/2 cup of bok choy heart centers (1/2 to 2 cups according to individual preference)
6 cups of chicken broth or mushroom seasoning with water (**See Dry Ingredients**)
1 1/2 Tbsp oil, oyster sauce, salt, sugar
Optional ingredients add color, texture, and variety to this vegetarian dish.

Soak the vermicelli in a bowl of hot water; drain and cut into thirds when it softens.
Save all the fragrant black mushroom water for soup.
Discard presoaked black mushroom stems and cut mushrooms into sixths.
Discard the hard stem ends of cloud ear mushrooms. Change water 3-4 times until water clears.
Discard water from cloud ear mushrooms.

Cut off and discard the green rind from the winter melon. Remove seeds. Use a pot just large enough to hold the piece of winter melon; pour enough chicken broth to cover the melon completely. Bring it to a boil and season to taste with salt. Cook on medium until tender (about 40 minutes.) If a wooden chopstick goes through the melon with ease, it is done. Take a small cutting of the winter melon to make sure it is very tender and tasty.

Stir-fry bok choy and black mushrooms in oil; add fried gluten, straw mushrooms, drained vermicelli, bamboo shoots, baby corn, lotus seeds, and 1 cup of chicken broth from the winter melon soup. Take out cooked bok choy centers so that it does not overcook while stir-frying the other vegetables for 10-15 minutes. Combine the bok choy with the vegetables and season to taste with salt, oyster sauce and sugar. Place the drained whole piece of winter melon in the middle of the serving dish and pour the vegetarian mix around the melon, showing the white round winter melon in the middle. The Winter Melon Vegetarian Gourmet is one of my favorite comfort foods. It's a **gourmet vegetarian** delight.

♥ Vegetarian Goose 素鵝

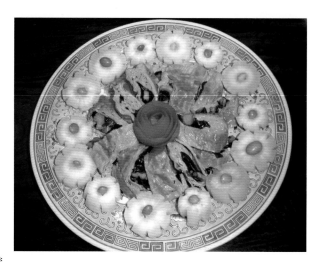

4 bean curd sheets (1/2 of a large 16-oz pkg from
the refrigerated section)
6-8 dried black mushrooms, presoaked and sliced,
with stems removed
1 large handful of dried cloud ear mushrooms,
presoaked, washed, and sliced
1/2 cup bamboo shoots (optional)
1/2 cup chicken broth
1 tsp light soy sauce, salt, pepper
Oyster sauce, 1 Tbsp oil
Marinade
1 1/4 cup chicken broth or use mushroom seasoning*
1 tsp light soy sauce, 1/2 tsp dark soy sauce
1 tsp sugar

See section on **Dry Ingredients** and **mushroom preparation** to save time.
Spread marinade on 4 bean sheets, turning the sheets over until they are soft and pliable.
Don't soak the sheets too long or it becomes difficult to wrap the rolls.

Sauté the two kinds of sliced mushrooms in 1 Tbsp oil; add 1 tsp light soy sauce, salt, pepper,
a little chicken broth, oyster sauce and sugar to taste. Set aside.
Take one large bean curd sheet and turn the round shape into a square by folding in the four
rounded edges towards the center. Put one column of the mushroom mixture on the square
shaped bean curd sheet, and start folding and rolling the mixture into a rounded column.
Set aside. Repeat with other sheets of bean curd and filling.

Steam Vegetarian Goose for 1 hr in a dish covered with wax paper and sealed with plastic wrap.
Chill. When ready to serve, slice the cold vegetarian goose into 1/2 inch diagonal pieces. This
is a terrific cold appetizer, or a delicious side dish. Extra rolls can be sealed in plastic wrap and
frozen until ready for serving. Defrost at least 3 hrs before serving. You can use 8 bean curd
sheets and double the other ingredients and freeze the extra rolls.

Enjoy. This is a delicious and nutritious low calorie dish, rich in protein and very pretty as an
appetizer or side dish. 4 sheets make 4 rolls of Vegetarian Goose. One roll cuts into 14 3/4-inch
slices. The bean curd sheets are also used for the **Steamed Vegetarian Rolls.**

Traditionally, tiger lilies are used as one of the main ingredients in Vegetarian Goose. However,
I deleted that from the recipe because it takes too long to prep the tiger lilies.

*Mushroom seasoning could be used as a substitute to chicken broth for strict vegetarians.
Mushroom seasoning does not have monosodium glutamate. Use about 1 tsp seasoning to one
cup of water. Mushroom seasoning can also be sprinkled on vegetables when stir-frying.
Use sparingly and add more if needed. **See photo on page 17.**

♥ Vegetarian Chicken 素 雞

1 Package frozen vegetarian chicken, 17.6 ozs
1 cup chicken broth or
1 1/2 tsp mushroom seasoning with 1 cup water
1 Tbsp oyster sauce or LKK Vegetarian Stir Fry Sauce

Dash of dark soy sauce
1 tsp tapioca starch or corn starch
1 tsp raw sugar
Dash of sesame seed oil

The vegetarian chicken is a substantial dish made of bean curd sheets that tastes like tofu. Look for it in the same section as the frozen bean curd knots.

Use a pot that is just big enough to hold the two pieces of vegetarian chicken. Parboil the vegetarian chicken in hot water. Rinse in cold water before cooking it in chicken broth or the equivalent of 1 cup water and 1 1/2 tsp mushroom seasoning. Bring broth to a boil and cook on low, covered, for 10 minutes until vegetarian chicken is done. Take out vegetarian chicken and let it cool before slicing into 1/4 inches.

Add a dash of dark soy sauce, sesame seed oil, and raw sugar to the remaining broth and season to taste with oyster sauce or LKK Vegetarian Stir Fry Sauce. Mix 1 tsp tapioca starch with 2 Tbsp broth and whisk into remaining hot broth over low heat to thicken the gravy. Reheat sliced vegetarian chicken in microwave and pour sauce over hot sliced vegetarian chicken. The **Photo** shows the package of frozen vegetarian chicken for easy identification of this food that only became recently available in some Chinese supermarkets.

This is a low calorie **Easy and Healthy** dish with great appeal to vegetarians. It is another variation of a tofu product.

♥ Steamed Vegetarian Rolls 蒸素卷

4 bean curd sheets, cut into 6-7 inch squares
1/2 head of napa cabbage, cut into 1 1/2 inch slivers
6 dried black mushrooms, presoaked 4 hrs or overnight, sliced, with stems removed
1 handful of dried cloud ear mushrooms, presoaked, washed, and sliced
Winter bamboo shoots, sliced thin
2-oz package of vermicelli, soaked in hot water, cut and drained
3 cloves of garlic, sliced
1tsp mushroom seasoning
Oyster sauce
2 Tbsp vegetable oil
Marinade
1 cup chicken broth
1 tsp light soy sauce
1/2 tsp dark soy sauce
1 tsp sugar

See section on **Dry Ingredients** and **mushroom preparation** to save time.

Heat wok on high, add oil, swirl oil, and stir-fry napa cabbage, garlic and mushrooms. Add 1tsp mushroom seaoning, vermicelli and bamboo shoots. Season to taste with salt, pepper, a little chicken broth and oyster sauce. When the cabbage is almost done, add sugar to taste. The chicken broth and juice from the vegetable should be evaporated. Set aside for wrapping.

Soak bean curd sheets in a marinade of 1 cup chicken broth, 1 tsp light and 1/2 tsp dark soy sauce, and a little sugar until sheets are wet and soft enough to wrap. Don't over-soak.

Put 1 Tbsp of the vegetarian mix on a sheet of bean curd and start wrapping the roll as in a mini package. Put the wrapped rolls into a 1 1/2 inches deep serving dish. Make another portion of marinade and pour on the wrapped rolls. Cover tightly and steam for an hour.
This makes a large portion which could be served in smaller quantities with sauce added.

Make a sauce with 1 1/2 cup of chicken broth mixed with a dash of oyster sauce and 1 Tbsp of corn starch to thicken the broth. Heat vegetarian rolls in broth when reheating so that the rolls will have a sauce. Add Chinese parsley or vegetarian garnish.

This is a low calorie dish that can be made ahead of time and reheated. The recipe serves 6-10. The bean sheets are also used for **Vegetarian Goose.**

❤ Broad Beans with Salted Mustard Greens 雪菜豆瓣

16 ozs frozen broad beans, shelled
1/2 cup of salted mustard greens, diced
3 cloves garlic, 1/2 -1 cup chicken broth

1/2 tsp mushroom seasoning
1 Tbsp Shaoxing cooking wine or pale dry sherry
Salt, 3 Tbsp sugar, 3 Tbsp oil

Sauté defrosted broad beans in oil, with garlic. Add mustard greens, wine, 1/2 cup of chicken broth, and mushroom seasoning. Sauté vegetables on medium heat until beans are tender. Add more chicken broth a little at a time as needed. Add sugar to taste. Broad beans call for more sugar than other vegetables.

This is an ethnic Shanghai-style vegetarian dish. Fresh broad beans in pods are not often found in grocery stores or markets and they need to be shelled. The fresh frozen broad beans are great substitutes that are delicious and a big time saver since they are already shelled. Young professionals who are too busy to scout for the vegetable and shell the fresh bean pods can appreciate the frozen broad beans. This is an **Easy, Healthy and Delicious** vegetarian dish.

❤ On Choy with Bean Curd 腐乳通菜

1 bunch On Choy
4-5 pieces of wet bean curd

5 cloves garlic, sliced
2 Tbsp oil, salt, white pepper, sugar

Use the leaves and only the tenderest small stems of the on choy branches, cut into 2-inch lengths. Wash and spin-dry the vegetable. Heat wok to high and add oil; stir fry on choy with garlic and bean curd. Mash bean curd while stir frying. Add salt, pepper and more bean curd if desired. Season to taste with a sprinkling of sugar.

The bean curd gives a lot of taste to the vegetable. On Choy cooks quickly within a few minutes. This is a favorite Cantonese vegetable and an **Easy, Healthy and Delicious** winner.

Variations: On Choy can be combined with stir-fried beef, chicken, shrimp, or canned Mexican shellfish, sliced. The vegetable is cooked the same way with 1 tsp of Double Deluxe Soy Sauce and 1 tsp mushroom seasoning in place of the bean curd, and topped with any of the meat and seafoods. The sliced shellfish does not need cooking.

♥ Buddha's Vegetarian Delight 羅漢齋

This is a traditional vegetarian dish for Chinese New Year. It is served during this holiday because prosperity vegetable is one of the must ingredients. Chinese are superstitious and enjoy foods that pun with "prosperity" and "consecutive sons" (for lotus seeds), thus starting the New Year with an auspicious beginning.

This is a simplified version of a traditional Buddha's Vegetarian Delight. Many dry ingredients are presoaked. Other than the variety of ingredients, the actual preparation is simply an assembly of all those ingredients.

8 dried black mushrooms, presoaked, stems removed, and cut into sixths
1/2 cup cloud ear mushrooms, presoaked and cleaned
1 cup canned straw mushrooms
1/2 cup dried prosperity vegetable, presoaked and rinsed
1 cup lotus seeds or gingko nut, purchased vacuum packed, refrigerated
1 bunch of baby bok choy, 1 cup baby corn
1 small package of mung bean vermicelli, presoaked, and cut into 3-inch lengths
1/2 cup sliced winter bamboo shoots
1 cup fresh baby carrots, sliced using the roll cutting method (See Basic Cutting Methods)
1 can of fried gluten with peanuts and mushrooms, sometimes called mock abalone
1/2 cup of fresh gluten, optional
Chicken broth, mushroom water, mushroom seasoning
5 cloves peeled, sliced garlic, 2-3 Tbsp vegetable oil
Oyster sauce, salt, white pepper, 2 Tbsp sugar

Check the section on **Dry Ingredients** with **Mushrooms** for presoaking, to save time in preparation. Presoak and prep the dry ingredients. Wash and cut bok choy into 1 inch pieces.

A large wok makes it easy to cook and assemble everything. Heat wok and stir-fry bok choy in oil; add mushrooms, baby carrots, salt, and white pepper. Set aside bok choy so that it does not get overcooked. Combine all the rest of the ingredients with chicken broth, and seasoning, putting bok choy back when all ingredients are cooked and assembled. There should not be any sauce, but enough chicken broth or mushroom water should be added to keep the vegetables moist while tossing the ingredients. Season to taste with salt, oyster sauce and sugar.

The key ingredient in this easy version of Buddha's Vegetarian Delight is the canned fried gluten, which has a delicious sauce which helps blend the ingredients. This recipe makes a large quantity which could be separated into several servings. A strict vegetarian should use mushroom seasoning instead of chicken broth. Serves 12. This is one of my favorite vegetarian dishes.

♥ Three Easy and Low Calorie Ways of Preparing Vegetables

Microwaved Green Vegetables

Wash and cut vegetables into serving pieces. Spin dry. Cover loosely with a piece of wax paper (so that the food cooks faster and more evenly.)
Microwave on high 1 1/2 -3 minutes. Certain vegetables cook faster and require less time. Vegetables should be slightly crunchy. You will discover the optimal time for cooking vegetables using this method.
Sauté microwaved green vegetable in 1 Tbsp hot oil and season to taste with salt, or soy sauce and a dash of sugar.
Skip the sautéing with oil if hot cooked vegetables are tossed in with the meats in the last minute when meat is almost cooked. Then season to taste.

Parboiled Vegetables in Chicken Broth

Bring chicken broth to a boil and toss in the vegetables with the pot lid off so that the vegetables stay green. Cook until the stems are tender, but not soggy. There should be some crunch to the vegetables. Drain and toss in with cooked meats or seafood that are already in the wok. Stir-fry a few seconds and season to taste. If you are cooking Chinese mustard greens, be sure to add extra sugar.

Parboiled Green Vegetables

This method of cooking vegetables works well only with Chinese broccoli, or gailan (with the very thick stems) and mustard greens, but never with regular broccoli.
Wash and cut vegetables into serving pieces. Bring a big pot of water to boil. Pour in 1 Tbsp salt, and parboil vegetables with a pinch of baking soda (1/8 tsp) for 2 min, or 'til tender and still slightly crunchy. Drain vegetables. Adding baking soda tenderizes the vegetable and decreases the cooking time while keeping the vegetable green.

Heat 1-2 Tbsp oil in the wok and toss parboiled vegetables with salt, soy sauce, and a dash of sugar. Or heat basic sauce in a small covered bowl and microwave for 1 minute on high. Toss with parboiled vegetables.
Basic Sauce: 1-2 Tbsp heated oil, 2 tsp light soy sauce, 1 1/2 tsp sugar

Soups

♥ Corn and Egg White Soup 雞茸粟米湯

1 15oz. can creamed corn,
3 egg whites, beaten until frothy
2 cloves garlic, sliced, 1 stalk scallion, diced
4 cups chicken broth

1 Tbsp Virginia ham, minced
1 Tbsp cornstarch, mixed with 1Tbsp water
Salt, white pepper
1 Tbsp Shaoxing cooking wine or pale dry sherry

Bring chicken broth and garlic slices to a boil; add corn and wine, and bring to a boil again. Add salt and pepper to taste.
In a small separate bowl, mix cornstarch with a little water until well blended. Pour the cornstarch mixture into the soup while stirring. This thickens the soup.

Stir well-beaten egg whites into the boiling broth. Stir again and bring to a boil. Add minced ham and scallions as garnish. Serves 6. This is an **Easy, Healthy and Delicious** Soup.

Drunken Clams 花雕醉蜆

12 Cherry Stone or Manila Clams
1 1/2 cups chicken broth, 1/2 cup water

1/4 cup of Shaoxing Hua Tiao wine
3 cloves garlic, 1 stalk scallion, diced

Choose live clams from the tank that have closed shells.

Brush and wash the clams thoroughly. Soak clams in a large pot of clear water, sprinkled with a little oil to clean out the sand inside the clams. Rinse many times in cold water until clear.

Heat chicken broth, wine, water, and garlic to a boil.   Throw in clams and cook on medium until clams open. As soon as the clam shell opens, it is done. As the shells open, take them out of the broth. Do not overcook clams or the meat will be tough. Discard any shells that do not open. Add scallions and season to taste.

♥ Winter Melon Soup 冬瓜湯

1 lb. winter melon   4 cups chicken broth
Virginia ham, slice 6-8 very thin pieces   3 cloves garlic, salt

Winter melon is most often sold in cut pieces. Rarely will you find a whole winter melon.
Cut and discard the green rind of the winter melon, remove the seeds, and slice melon into
approximately 1 1/2 inch by 1 inch by 1/2 inch thick pieces.

Cook winter melon with ham slices and garlic in chicken broth, with enough liquid to cover
sliced melon. Bring everything to a boil; then cook on low until winter melon is tender, about
20-25 minutes. Season to taste.
The Winter Melon Soup is an **Easy, Healthy and Delicious** soup that can be prepared in half
an hour. Serves 4-6

♥ Bamboo Pith and Mushroom Soup 竹笙冬菇湯

10 pieces of bamboo pith, presoaked 2 days ahead
6 black mushrooms, presoaked for 4 hrs or overnight
6 slices of Virginia ham, thin slices
2 pieces of dried scallops, soaked and hand shredded to thin slivers
3 stalks scallions, 2 cloves garlic, 3 slices ginger
6 cups Chicken Broth

The key to the success of this soup is to use the best chicken broth. See **Prime Chicken Broth.**
If you don't have time to make **Prime Chicken Broth**, use canned chicken broth.

Soak bamboo pith in water, and change water until it is clear. Sprinkle a tablespoon of salt in
the water to help get rid of some of the yellow color in the water during the last rinse. Change
water again to get rid of salt. Trim the ends of the bamboo pith, and use only the whole pieces.
Cut into 3-inch lengths for the soup and save the rest for vegetable dishes.

Boil chicken broth and the water used to soak the scallops. Add sliced Virginia ham, dried
scallops, garlic, ginger, and scallions; simmer for 45 minutes. Add whole mushrooms and
bamboo pith; bring contents to a boil and simmer for 30-40 minutes. Discard ginger, garlic,
and scallions. Serve hot soup in a large tureen or individual bowls.
Serves 6-8.

Buddha Jumps the Wall

Ingredients for Buddha Jumps the Wall
1. Canned Abalone Type Shellfish from Mexico
2. Canned Whole Baby Abalone
3. Dried Scallops
4. Hua Tiao Cooking Wine
5. Dried Fish Maw
6. Frozen Sea Cucumber
7. Buddha Jumps the Wall served in a large soup bowl
8. Steamed soup in small individual soup bowls
9. Steamed Chicken in a clay pot steamer

Buddha Jumps the Wall 佛跳牆

There is a charming story that goes with this delicious soup. Buddha was walking down the street holding his prayer beads when he sniffed a fantastic aroma of food that came from a restaurant. Without any hesitation, he followed his nose, jumped over the wall and landed in the back yard of the restaurant. The broth was so deliciously tempting that even Buddha was willing to break his vegetarian diet to sample the heavenly soup. That was how the soup got its name.

8 cups of prime chicken broth, 4 Tbsp Hua Tiao wine
6 pieces of dried scallop, soaked in water overnight and shredded to fine slivers by hand
1 large piece or 10 small pieces of dried fish maw 魚膠, soaked in water for 3-4 days
1 lb package of frozen small sea cucumber (small is preferable)
6 cloves garlic, 1 small piece of peeled ginger, 2 stalks scallions
1/2 cup of winter bamboo shoots, sliced thin
8 dried black mushrooms, presoaked 4 hrs or overnight
1 can of shellfish (12-13 Australian baby abalone or Mexican "abalone type" shellfish)
Sesame oil, salt and pepper

Steam dried scallops, covered, in soaking water for 90 minutes ahead of time. Large fish maw is very thick, more desirable and quite expensive. Fish maw needs to be presoaked and cleaned thoroughly to get rid of sand. Parboil fish maw and sea cucumber in a large pot of water. Drain and rinse in cold water. Steam, covered, the chicken broth, juice from soaking the dried scallops, and first 5 ingredients. Steam 60-90 minutes until the fish maw and sea cucumber are tender. If large fish maw and large sea cucumber are used, cut into serving pieces and allow more time for steaming. The small variety steams very quickly and dissolves if over-steamed. Add to the soup whole baby abalone or Mexican type shellfish, sliced thin, sliced mushrooms, bamboo shoots, and the juice from the can of shellfish and steam 30 minutes more. Discard ginger and scallions. Season to taste.

This is a gourmet soup that is served in a few Chinese restaurants. They include sharks fins as one of the ingredients. I have deleted that from our ingredients after hearing how the fishermen catch sharks just for their fins. The live sharks are thrown back into the sea with no chance of survival after the fins are cut. I understand that many young people in Thailand are boycotting sharks fins, even though it is a favorite delicacy. If you want to include sharks fins, get the small frozen crescent shaped fins. Parboil the fins; rinse and simmer in broth for about 30-40 minutes with the rest of the ingredients until tender.

Buddha Jumps the Wall is a **gourmet soup** fit for the most discriminating epicurean. The soup is fantastic even without the shark's fins. For company, use Australian baby abalone instead of Mexican "abalone type " shellfish. Serves 8-10.
See Photo of Ingredients for Buddha Jumps the Wall.

♥ Steamed Chicken in a Clay Pot Steamer 氣鍋雞

Diagram of clay pot steamer
on a pot of boiling water

Inside view with steam vent

This soup is cooked in a clay pot steamer with a vent that allows steam to rise into the pot and cook the food inside the clay pot while the steam condenses and makes a delicious pure broth. It is well worth the effort getting this special pot for a heavenly soup and tender chicken. Clay pot steamers are made with either a centre steam vent or side steam vents. The latter type is preferable because it holds more soup.

8 chicken drumsticks
6 dried black mushrooms, presoaked
2 stalks scallions, 2 cloves garlic
1 large piece ginger, sliced, salt, white pepper
1 Tbsp Shaoxing cooking wine or pale dry sherry

Discard skin and chop chicken into 1 1/2 inch pieces. Wash and drain.
Marinate chicken with 1/2 tsp salt, white pepper, garlic, ginger, and scallions for a few hours or overnight.
Fill the clay steamer half full with seasoned chicken, mushrooms with stems removed, mushroom water (from soaking the black mushrooms,) ginger, garlic, scallions, and wine.
Add enough water to cover the chicken and mushrooms, leaving about 1/3 inch for the steam to condense into soup.

Put the clay pot steamer on a deep pot of boiling water and steam for 3 hours on medium heat. Set a timer to add boiling water to the pot below. The clay pot steamer has to sit directly and tightly above the pot so that it catches all the steam evaporating from the pot of water below. Remove ginger, scallions and garlic, and skim off the chicken fat on top. Season to taste with salt. Serves 4-6.
The steamed chicken and mushrooms are tender and the soup is clear, pure, and supremely delicious. Serve the **Easy, Healthy and Delicious** Steamed Chicken piping hot.

Steamed Whole Winter Melon 燉冬瓜盅

1 whole winter melon, 1/2 cup crabmeat
1/2 cup chicken breast, cut into 1/4" cubes
1/2 cup lean pork loin, cut into 1/4" cubes
3/4 cup black mushrooms, presoaked, 1/4" cubes
2 dried scallops, soaked overnight, shredded
1/4 can of small straw mushrooms, drained
1/4 cup Virginia ham, cut into 1/4" cubes
2 cups of prime chicken broth
1/4 cup winter bamboo shoots, cut into 1/4" cubes
1/2 cup crabmeat
2 pieces of scallions, 2 cloves garlic, salt
1 Tbs Shaoxing wine or pale dry sherry

This is a **gourmet feast dish** that is served at banquets and big dinner parties. A hollowed out winter melon serves as the container for cooking and serving this delicious soup. Choose a small whole melon that will fit into a stock pot. The melon has to sit in a bowl that will hold the entire melon while being steamed in the stock pot for 4-5 hours. The bowl sits on a low rack. It will take some effort to find the right size melon that will hold sufficient soup and still fit into a covered stock pot. My pot is 12 1/2 inches in diameter x 10 inches high.

Save the water from soaking the dried mushrooms and dried scallops for the soup. Use a sharp knife, cutting at a 45 degree angle, to carve out a round circle on top of the melon. Remove the cut portion and keep the top for a cover. Scoop out the seeds and the white center near the seeds. Save the white center and cut into cubes.

Fill the bottom of the melon with the water from the mushrooms and dried scallops. Add the cubes and all the above cut ingredients, except the crab meat and straw mushrooms. Fill the rest of the melon with water up to 3/4 full, leaving about one inch down from the top, to allow for condensation of steam to seep into the soup. Put the original lid back on the melon; it will be a perfect fit.

Fill the stock pot with water up to the halfway mark of the bowl holding the melon. Bring the water to a boil, and turn to low. Steam 4-5 hours, checking periodically to make sure there is enough water in the stock pot. The soup is ready when the white portion of the melon is translucent. In the last 30 minutes, remove scallions and garlic, add crab meat and straw mushrooms and season to taste with salt. Steam 10 minutes. The broth will be delicious, so it needs only very light seasoning.

Wearing gloves, lift the bowl holding the melon out of the cooking pot and serve it whole. Scoop the melon and soup ingredients into individual soup bowls. At restaurants, the chef sometimes carves elaborate decorations on the melon. But for home dinners, the whole melon is beautiful without any decorations and is a special treat.

Simplified Winter Melon Soup 燉冬瓜茸

This is a simplified method of preparing the Steamed Whole Winter Melon. The taste is similar but you save yourself the trouble of having to find a huge pot that would hold the entire melon. It is still a delicious soup with the same ingredients, but it can be prepared more easily. See Section on Dry Ingredients and Mushroom Preparation to save time.

1 large section of winter melon
3 cups of chicken broth
1/2 cup chicken breast, cut into 1/4 inch cubes
1/2 cup lean pork loin, cut into 1/4 inch cubes
1/2 cup black mushrooms, presoaked, and cut into 1/4 inch pieces (save water for soup)
2 pieces of dried scallops, soaked overnight and shredded into smaller pieces by hand
1/2 cup canned straw mushrooms, discard water from canned mushrooms
1/4 cup Virginia ham, cut into 1/4 inch cubes
1/2 cup crabmeat
1/4 cup winter bamboo shoots cut into 1/4 inch cubes
2 stalks scallions, 2 cloves garlic
Salt, white pepper
1 Tbsp Shaoxing wine or pale dry sherry

Save the water from the dried mushrooms and dried scallops for the winter melon soup.
Cut the green rind off and dice the winter melon into 1/2 inch cubes. Set aside.
Put all the above ingredients (except the melon, crab meat, straw mushrooms and bamboo shoots) into a large deep soup bowl with 2 cups of boiling water, chicken broth, saved mushroom and scallop water. Cover the soup bowl tightly so that water cannot seep into the bowl; place soup bowl on a rack and steam in a large pot of boiling water for 2 hrs until the meat is tender. Add melon cubes, straw mushrooms, bamboo shoots and steam for approximately 1-2 hours or until winter melon is done.
Add crabmeat 3 minutes before serving. Season to taste. Be sure to set the timer and add hot boiling water periodically to the pot so that it does not run out of water during the steaming.

This is a **delicious gourmet soup** prepared with less fuss and fanfare than its aristocratic cousin, using a whole winter melon.

Soup and Dinner in a Casserole 醃篤鮮

1 whole chicken, or 6 drumsticks and 6 thighs
1/2 lb lean pork, cut into 1/2 inch cubes
Virginia ham bone and 12 slices of ham
6-8 pieces of salted dried bamboo shoots, cut into 2 inch lengths（鹹筍）
6-8 dried black mushrooms, presoaked for 4 hrs or overnight
8 slices of dried shellfish, optional
8-oz package of frozen sheet bean curd knots（百頁）
l piece ginger, peeled, 6 cloves garlic
salt, dash of white pepper
1/8 tsp baking soda
3 Tbsp Shaoxing cooking wine or pale dry sherry
Napa Chinese cabbage, washed and cut into 1 1/2 inch pieces
sliced winter bamboo shoots, optional

Parboil bean curd knots with baking soda in boiling water for 2 minutes. Rinse in cold water, drain and set aside. The frozen bean curd knots are tenderized with baking soda. If you buy the refrigerated white bean curd knots (rather than the frozen variety), then don't parboil with baking soda since the texture is already very soft. I prefer the frozen.

Bring 3qts (12 cups) of water to a boil in a large pot; put in chicken, pork and bean curd knots. When adding new ingredients to a soup, always bring the contents to a boil, then reduce heat. If a whole chicken is used, be sure the water covers the entire chicken. Skim off the scum as it rises to the surface. Add ham, sliced shellfish, ginger, salted dried bamboo shoots, salt, pepper, wine. Bring to a boil and reduce heat to low; simmer 4 hrs. Skim off the fat.

Add mushrooms, napa cabbage, and sliced winter bamboo shoots. Bring to a boil and then turn to low and cook for an hour. Season to taste.

The lean pork and ham add a lot of flavor, but the soup can be made with only chicken for those who prefer not to eat pork. I cook the chicken without the skin, but that is a personal choice. The bean curd knots and vegetables are irresistibly delicious. It's a nutritious and easy slow cooked soup and dinner all in one.

Prime Chicken Broth 上湯

This is the basic chicken broth that is used to make soups. Good chicken broth makes vegetables and a myriad of other dishes taste wonderful. It is a big advantage if you have space in the freezer to store prime chicken broth in small containers. On the other hand, if time and space are considerations, you could use low-sodium canned chicken broth, chicken essence, or mushroom seasoning as substitutes.

1 whole chicken
chicken or pork bones
1/2 lb lean pork, cut into 1 inch pieces
ham bone, if available
1 piece ginger, peeled

8 cloves garlic
3 scallions
1 cup dried salted bamboo (鹹荀)
Salt

Fill a large stock pot with 2 1/2 gallons of water that amply covers the whole chicken, Bring all the ingredients to a boil, skim off the scum on the surface, and cook on low for 4 hours. Discard ginger, scallions and garlic, and season to taste with more salt. Let the broth cool and skim off the chicken fat on top. Pour strained soup into smaller containers for freezing. Plastic half-gallon ice cream and yogurt containers are very handy.

When you are ready to use the broth, defrost and skim off remaining chicken fat again before using the broth. Prime chicken broth is pure and delicious and better than commercial soup because it does not have monosodium glutamate and other ingredients that are used to enhance taste.

For those who prefer not to use pork or ham, it's okay to use just chicken with the other ingredients and decrease the water by a gallon.

The meat and dried salted bamboo can be used for soup.

Vegetable Rice, Shanghai Style

Rice & Noodles, Snacks

Shanghai style Vegetable Rice 菜飯

The traditional way of making this regional dish is with pork, ham, sausages, and bok choy stir fried in a lot of oil and simmered in rice. This is a simplified, low calorie version of Vegetable Rice, Shanghai Style, that has the aroma and fragrance of comfort food from Shanghai.

2 cups long grain rice, chicken broth
2 bunches of bok choy
1/4 cup of Virginia ham, sliced thin, then diced (or small dried shrimp)
1 link Chinese pork sausage, steamed and diced (optional)
2-3 Tbsp vegetable oil, 5 cloves garlic, minced
Salt, white pepper, sugar
1 tsp mushroom seasoning (optional)
See photo of Dry Ingredients

Steam pork sausage for 40 minutes. Cool and dice into 1/4 inch cubes. Cook rice and diced ham using chicken broth instead of water in the exact proportion as you would ordinarily in an electric rice cooker, less 4 Tbsp of liquid. Use the measuring cup that comes with the electric rice cooker (equivalent to 3/4 cup standard measuring cup) to measure the rice.

Wash and cut bok choy into 1/2 inch pieces. Use a lot of vegetables, about one bunch or 2 full cups of chopped bok choy to each cup of rice.
Stir-fry 4 cups of chopped bok choy with minced garlic in a generous amount of oil. Season with salt, pepper, and sugar to taste. Add mushroom seasoning (optional) if you want more flavor in the vegetables. Cook until most of the liquid is evaporated. The vegetable is cooked but not soggy. Add steamed diced sausage.

When the rice cooker light goes off, or when there are approximately 12 minutes left for the rice in the rice cooker, add the bok choy and meats. Mix well with the rice. Let the vegetables and meats simmer for another 20-30 minutes.

Serve the vegetable rice piping hot. This makes about 6 bowls of rice. Those who prefer not to use ham and sausage can substitute 1/4 cup of small dried shrimp, added to the rice when you start the rice cooker. The bok choy is prepared the same way as above and added later. I do not ordinarily eat rice with dinner, but I always have a second helping of Vegetable Rice. Vegetable Rice is an **Easy, Healthy and Delicious** recipe you'll love.

Rice Porridge with Preserved Eggs 皮蛋瘦肉粥

3/4 cup rice, 2 Tbsp sweet rice (glutinous rice)
1/2 lb lean pork (boneless)
3 preserved duck eggs
5 cloves garlic, 2 stalks scallions, diced
Salt, white pepper

1 tsp mushroom seasoning
Oyster sauce
1 Tbsp Shaoxing wine or pale dry sherry
Fresh Chinese parsley for garnish

Marinate pork (leave it in one whole piece) with 2 tsp salt overnight.
Boil 10 cups of water in a large pot, and add rice, sweet rice, pork, garlic, salt, pepper, and wine. Bring contents to a boil again; then turn the heat down and simmer for 3 1/2 hrs, until the rice is soft, and the rice grains split open.

The porridge is ready when the liquid is glutinous and the pork is so tender that you could put a chopstick right through the meat. You use a large pot so that the porridge will not boil over and make a mess.

Take out the pork and shred it in a bowl to small slivers. The pork is very tender and shreds easily with a knife or spoon. Put the shredded pork back into the porridge. Season to taste with salt, pepper, 1 tsp of mushroom seasoning and a dash of oyster sauce. Cut preserved eggs into small quarter inch pieces and add to porridge along with diced scallions. Garnish with Chinese parsley. Serve hot.

This is a Cantonese favorite, often served with Dim Sum in restaurants. It could be served for breakfast, lunch, or snack.
Using the microwave to reheat individual portions of porridge safeguards the porridge from scorching. An easy alternate method of making the rice porridge is to use a large crock pot with the same ingredients using 10 cups of liquid and cook on auto overnight; then shred the pork and add the eggs and two cups of boiling water the next morning. I like this method because it is easy and the crock pot creates no mess. This is an **Easy and Delicious** breakfast or snack food. Serves 10.
Add more boiling water if you like a thin rice porridge. Extra porridge can be frozen, or reduce ingredients proportionally to make smaller quantity.

♥ Rice Porridge with Fish Filet 魚片粥

3/4 cup rice, 2 Tbsp sweet rice (glutinous rice)
10 cups chicken broth, or 10 tsp of mushroom seasoning with 10 cups of water
2 pieces fish filet (bass or sole), cut into 1/4 inch slices for 4-6 bowls of porridge
2 stalks scallions, diced, 3 cloves garlic, salt, pepper
1 Tbsp Shaoxing wine or pale dry sherry
1/2 cup roasted peanuts, optional
Dash of pure sesame seed oil, optional

In a large pot, bring the broth to a boil and add both kinds of rice, garlic, and wine. Bring back to a boil, reduce heat and simmer on low for 3 hours until the rice is soft and the porridge is glutinous.
It is important to use a large pot that is big enough so that the porridge does not bubble over and make a mess. Just before serving, add sliced fish and scallions to hot porridge and simmer for two minutes. The fish and scallions cook almost instantly. Sprinkle with a dash of sesame oil, and season to taste with salt, pepper, and a dash of oyster sauce. Serve with a dish of crunchy peanuts.

A simple alternate method of cooking the rice porridge is to use a large crock pot and cook overnight on Auto using the same ingredients. Add boiling water to hot porridge if you want a lighter consistency to the porridge just before serving. Stir sliced fish into the hot bubbling porridge and season to taste the same way.
I prefer this method of making porridge because it is easy and the crock pot creates no mess. You will love this **Easy, Healthy and Delicious** recipe.

This could be served for breakfast, lunch, or a late night snack. Cook enough fish that can be consumed in one meal; this way the fish will always be tender. There will be plenty of plain rice porridge left to try numerous variations.

Variations to Rice Porridge Make Great Companion Meals:
Beef Rice Porridge: See recipe
Chicken Rice Porridge : Use sliced chicken filet from any of the chicken filet entrées to create this companion dish in the same way as the Beef Rice Porridge the next day.
Seafood Rice Porridge: Add diced shrimp and fish filet, raw and marinated, and diced scallions to boiling rice porridge the same way as the Beef Rice Porridge.
Plain Rice Porridge served with roasted peanuts and shredded roast pork or shredded fish (肉鬆 or魚鬆) See Picture of Preparing Vietnamese Spring Rolls to see the dry ingredient (肉鬆).

Beef Rice Noodles, A 10-Minute Companion Dish

1/4 cup sliced beef flank steak
1 section of rice noodles
1 cup baby bok choy, or pre-washed spinach, or other seasonal vegetables
1/2 cup canned straw mushrooms (optional)
2 1/2 cups chicken broth (or 2 1/2 tsp of mushroom seasoning with 2 1/2 cups water)
Dash of LKK double deluxe soy sauce, white pepper

When you make the Beef with Fresh Green Vegetables, put aside 1/4 cup marinated and seasoned sliced beef and create a delicious companion dish for lunch that can be made in less than 10 minutes the next day.

Parboil rice noodles in boiling water for three minutes; drain and cook rice noodles with cut baby bok choy in chicken broth until vegetables are tender, not overcooked or soggy.

Slice beef to thin slivers and add a dash of double deluxe soy sauce. Whisk into boiling broth with rice noodles. If spinach is used, add in the last minute, stir, season to taste, and serve immediately. Enjoy an **Easy, Healthy and Delicious** bowl of rice noodles. 1-2 servings

Beef Rice Porridge, A 5-minute Companion Dish

1/4 cup sliced beef flank steak, slivered thin
Make rice porridge in crock pot the night before (See rice porridge)
1 egg (optional)
1 stalk scallions, diced
Dash of Double Deluxe Soy Sauce
Dash of sesame oil, white pepper

The Beef Rice Porridge is a variation to the Beef Rice Noodles that is just as simple. When you make the Beef with Fresh Green Vegetables, put aside 1/4 cup marinated and seasoned sliced beef to create a delicious companion dish for lunch that can be made in 5 minutes the next day.

Make rice porridge in a crock pot the night before. Next day, pour 6 cups of hot porridge into a separate pot. Mix slivered beef with a dash of double deluxe sauce and whisk into bubbling hot porridge; add a fresh egg, and stir until the white of the egg turns white and beef is barely done. Add a dash of sesame oil, white pepper, and scallions. Serve immediately. Enjoy an **Easy. Healthy and Delicious** rice porridge with beef that is as tender as filet mignon. Save remainder of rice porridge in the crock pot for another companion dish: Chicken Rice Porridge or Fish Rice Porridge.

The rice porridge or soup noodles can be made with sliced chicken filet in the same way.

Noodle Topping: Chicken with Mushrooms and yellow chives

1. Rice sticks for soup noodles 2. Round cakes of noodles from Yee county
3. Shrimp flavored noodles for soup or fried noodles.

Noodles with Crab Meat 韭黃蟹肉伊麵

1/2 package of Yee noodles
1/4 cup crab meat, 1/2 cup of yellow chives, cut into 2"
3 cups chicken broth or 3 cups water with 3 tsp mushroom seasoning
1 Tbsp oil, sesame oil

Noodles from Yee County are delicious. They are packaged like twin hat boxes.
Parboil one portion of the round kegs of noodles in boiling water and drain.

Bring chicken broth to a boil, (or 3 cup of water to boil with 3 tsp mushroom seasoning.). Add parboiled noodles and cook 2 minutes. Sauté crab meat and yellow chives in oil for one minute, and season to taste with salt and a dash of sesame oil; pour on top of soup noodles.   Recipe makes 1 large bowl of delicious soup noodles or 2 medium servings.

Fried Noodles with Chicken, Chives, and Mushrooms
韭黃銀芽雞絲炒麵

3-4 pieces of dried shrimp noodles
Leftover noodle topping: Chicken, mushrooms, bean sprouts
2 Tbsp oil, salt, pepper, Dash oyster sauce
1/2 tsp LKK double deluxe soy sauce
1/2 cup fresh yellow chives, 2" pieces

This is my husband's favorite noodles for lunch. I make this if I have a portion of the Chicken with Mushrooms and Bean Sprouts already set aside from the previous dinner.

Parboil the shrimp-flavored noodles (3-4 oval pieces of dried noodles) in hot water for
3 minutes.
Separate the noodles and rinse in cold water. Drain well.
Heat 2 Tbsp of oil in a wok and stir-fry noodles. Season with salt, white pepper, 1/2 tsp of light soy sauce, and a dash of oyster sauce to taste. Place on serving plate.
Toss the already prepared chicken and mushrooms in the wok; add the chopped yellow chives; toss in wok for 2 minutes and serve on top of fried noodles.

Many stir-fried shrimp, beef, chicken and vegetarian dishes can do double duty as entrées and noodle toppings just by making slightly larger portions and setting them aside for soup or fried noodles. **See photo of noodle topping.**

♥ Soup Rice Noodles with Chicken, Mushrooms, and Bean Sprouts 雞絲湯米粉

The easiest way to enjoy the soup rice noodles with Chicken, Mushrooms and Bean Sprouts is to serve it when you have already set aside a cup of the sautéed chicken from dinner for the noodle topping. Parboil 1 portion of rice noodles in boiling water (4 portions in a package.) Drain and rinse in cold water. Bring 2 1/2 cups of chicken broth (or use mushroom seasoning and water) to a boil; add parboiled noodles and cook 2 minutes. Serve rice noodles with Chicken, Mushroom, and Bean Sprout topping.

Ingredients for the Chicken, Mushrooms, and Bean Sprouts
1/2 skinless boned chicken breast, sliced and slivered into the size of match sticks
4 black mushrooms, presoaked for 4 hrs or overnight, and sliced
Winter bamboo shoots (optional) sliced thin
1/2 lb fresh bean sprouts, parboiled just a minute
3 cloves garlic, salt and pepper, 2 Tbsp oil
1 1/2 tsp cornstarch
1 tsp Shaoxing cooking wine or pale dry sherry
1/2 tsp light soy sauce
Oyster sauce

Slice whole chicken filet lengthwise into thin long pieces. Then cut sliced chicken against the grain into slivers about the size of match sticks.

Marinate chicken with garlic, cornstarch, wine, salt, and pepper. Heat wok until it's very hot. Pour oil in wok, swirl oil and stir fry chicken and garlic on high. Add mushrooms, bamboo shoots (optional,) parboiled bean sprouts, and light soy sauce. Season to taste with salt, oyster sauce, and a sprinkling of sugar. Serve hot.

The Chicken, Mushroom, and Bean Sprouts could be a main dish or a noodle topping and is one of the main ingredients in the Vietnamese Style Spring Rolls.
Many other stir-fried chicken, beef, and shrimp dishes can be used for noodle topping.

Rice Stuffing for Turkey 糯米飯

1/4 lb lean pork, diced into 1/4 inch squares
1 link Chinese pork sausage, steamed for 20 min and diced
1/4 cup diced Virginia ham (optional)
8 dried black mushrooms, presoaked 4 hrs or overnight and diced into 1/4" squares
1/4 cup dried shrimp, small
8-10 ozs. chestnuts, pre-roasted and shelled (optional)
2 cups sweet rice (glutinous rice), use measuring cup which comes with rice cooker
Chicken broth, 1 tsp corn starch
2 tsp light soy sauce, salt, pepper, 4 cloves garlic, sliced
1 tsp Shaoxing cooking wine or pale dry sherry
1 Tbsp oil, canola oil spray (optional)

Cook the rice in a rice cooker using chicken broth instead of water. Before starting the rice, reduce broth by 4 Tbsp. Mushroom seasoning can be used as a substitute for chicken broth. See section on Dry Ingredients p 17.

Look for pre-roasted, shelled, peeled, and ready to eat chestnuts, available in Chinese supermarkets. If you cannot find the ready to eat chestnuts, get the frozen or dried ones and cook in chicken broth for 20-40 minutes until tender. Cut the cooked chestnuts in half.

Mix pork with soy sauce, salt, pepper, wine, and cornstarch.
Heat wok on high until it's very hot. Pour oil in wok, swirl oil, and stir-fry pork and garlic. Add soy sauce, mushrooms, Virginia ham, sausage, dried shrimp, and 2 Tbsp mushroom water, and cook on medium heat for about 10-15 minutes or until the meat is barely cooked. Add cooked rice, chestnuts, and a little oyster sauce and mix well. Set aside. As a precautionary measure, don't stuff the turkey until you are ready to bake the bird. Never leave a stuffed uncooked fowl at room temperature.

The rice stuffing is made ahead of time and set aside. Rinse the turkey in cold water and season the cavity and skin with salt, pepper, and garlic. Put rice stuffing in the turkey; spray the skin with canola oil, and bake immediately.
A short cut is to bake the turkey in a Reynolds Oven Cooking Bag as it reduces the cooking time in half and saves the trouble of basting. Follow bake instructions for the bag, and the turkey comes out tender with all the juice collected in the bag. Skim the fat off the juice.

Extra rice stuffing could be baked in foil with the turkey. My family enjoys the rice stuffing almost more than the turkey. This rice stuffing could stuff either chicken or duck. The traditional rice stuffing is made without the chestnuts. You will find that the addition of chestnuts make the stuffing irresistibly delicious.

Chestnuts with Jewelled Rice 栗子糯米飯

2 cups Sweet Rice (glutinous rice, use measuring cup which comes with rice cooker)
8-10 ozs roasted shelled and peeled chestnuts (ready to eat)
Chicken broth or mushroom seasoning (See Dry Ingredients)
8 dried black mushrooms, presoaked for 4 hrs or overnight
2 Tbsp small dried shrimp
2 Tbsp thinly diced Virginia ham
1 link pork sausage, steamed for 20 minutes, diced
1 Tbsp oyster sauce, 1 tsp soy sauce, pepper and garlic powder
3 cloves garlic, minced
1 Tbsp vegetable oil

Cook rice in a rice cooker using chicken broth instead of water; before starting the rice cooker, reduce broth by 4 Tbsp. If you are measuring 3 cups of rice, then reduce broth by 6 Tbsp. Alternatively, you can use mushroom seasoning instead of chicken broth. The measuring cup that comes with the rice cooker is equivalent to 3/4 cup standard measuring cup.

Remove stems of mushrooms and cut mushrooms into 1/4 inch squares. Use a Teflon pan to sauté diced mushrooms and garlic in 1Tbsp hot oil; add dried shrimp, diced ham, steamed and diced sausage, and season lightly with oyster sauce. Cut chestnuts into quarters and add to mixture.

When the light goes off on the rice cooker (12 minutes before the rice is ready,) add the diced meats and chestnuts to the rice and mix well. Let the rice simmer in the cooker for 20 minutes or longer.   Serve the delicious rice right out of the cooker or you can wrap it in a large piece of lotus leaf and steam for 20-30 minutes. The recipe can be doubled.to serve 8-10.

The sausage and ham add a lot of flavor to the rice, but those ingredients can be substituted by using additional mushrooms and dried shrimp.

The Chestnuts with Jeweled Rice is an Easy and Delicious rice that everyone will love. This is a fantastic recipe that can be prepared in half an hour; the rice cooker will do the rest.

Roasted Candied Pecans & Mabel's Roasted Peanuts

♥ Roasted Candied Pecans 糖胡桃

2 cups pecan halves
1 cup light brown sugar

Boil 1 3/4 quarts of water in a large 2 quart pot. Then blanch pecans and turn off the range.
Wait 4 minutes and drain water thoroughly in a colander.
Melt light brown sugar with drained pecans and stir over medium heat until nuts are coated and
the sugar begins to caramelize, about two minutes.   Drain thoroughly.

Spread pecans in one layer on parchment lined cookie sheet. Bake 1hr @ 275 degrees preheated
oven. Turn pecans and bake 1 hr @ 170 degrees. Shake and bake 1 hr longer. Turn off oven
and leave overnight without opening the oven door. Ovens vary in temperature; increase bake
time to make pecans crispier. The **Easy, Healthy and Delicious** pecans are light and crunchy.

♥ Mabel's Roasted Peanuts　烤花生

2 bags peanuts (raw shelled, 12-14 ozs each)
1/4 cup sugar
1/4 cup salt (less 1Tbsp)
2 cups water
8 star anise

Bring water to a boil with the spices, salt and sugar. Add peanuts and cook 5 minutes or until liquid boils again. Drain in a colander.

Spread peanuts on cookie sheet or roasting pan in one layer. Roast @230 degrees for 90-120 minutes. Turn off oven and leave overnight without opening the oven door. Store peanuts in a jar. Depending on your oven, if you like the peanuts to be more crunchy, you could increase the roasting time but not the oven temperature. The star anise is reusable.
These **Easy, Healthy and Delicious** roasted peanuts are irresistible.

♥ Candied Pinenuts　松子糖

2 cups of pine nuts
1 large egg white
1 cup powdered sugar

Beat egg whites, and 4 Tbsp sugar until frothy. Mix 4 Tbsp sugar with nuts; add pine nuts to egg white mixture and spread in 1 layer on heavy foil. Bake in a preheated oven for 4 minutes @ 325 degrees. Turn and separate nuts and bake another minute. Sprinkle remaining sugar gradually while stirring and separating the moist nuts until they are crispy and completely coated. Store in jars when nuts are cooled. This is a dainty **Easy, Healthy and Delicious** snack that originated in Shanghai.

♥ Ginger Milk Pudding 薑汁奶

1 large piece of old ginger with crusty peel	2 Tbsp sugar
2-2 1/2 cups whole or 2% low fat milk	Thermometer

This is SK, my cookbook sponsor's favorite milk pudding. He described the pudding to me and the way that it is made in Hong Kong. I was not sure I had enough time to decode the enigma of making the ginger milk gel. Luckily, several friends enthusiastically helped me figure out this amazing recipe, which is made with ginger juice and milk. We made many futile attempts before achieving success.

While in NYC visiting our granddaughter, I found a restaurant that served the ginger milk pudding. After I sampled a variation of it with egg white, I went to the kitchen with renewed confidence, knowing how it should taste. I followed Louise Yu's revised instructions, and this time, it worked like a charm.

Peel ginger and use a food processor to shred ginger into pulp. You can use a microplane grater, but the food processor is much easier. Use a fine sieve or gauze to filter 2 tsp of fresh ginger juice for every 8-10 ozs of milk. Be sure to include the white residue that settles to the bottom of the ginger juice as it helps gel the pudding. Heat 1Tbsp sugar with 8-10 ozs of milk in a pyrex pitcher and microwave for about 2 1/2 minutes until sugar is dissolved and milk forms small bubbles on the sides, but is not boiling. The strength of microwaves can vary so use a thermometer to ensure the temperature of milk is between 171-178 degrees Fahrenheit or 77 degrees Centigrade so the milk will gel. It is easier to pour by making single portions and pour into bowls or coffee mugs. It is also easier to make the milk gel when unpeeled ginger is left at room temperature for at least 2 weeks. Make fresh ginger juice just before you make the pudding.

Put 2 tsp ginger juice in each serving bowl and place bowls in a sink to collect any splattering milk. Swirl ginger juice in bowl and pour 8-10 ounces of the hot milk mixture into each serving bowl from a height of about 10 inches above the bowl. The ginger milk will congeal in one minute. It's a light, nutritious, and delicate pudding that is quite unique to most Western tastes but very popular in certain parts of the Far East. Serve hot or cold.

Egg White and Ginger Milk Pudding is a variation to the Ginger Milk Pudding that is served in some Dim Sum restaurants. That was the sample that I tried in NYC and having tasted the pudding, I gained enough confidence to try remaking the pudding. If the ginger milk does not gel, then whisk 1 beaten egg white into 4-41/2 cups of warm ginger milk mixture in a bowl (or 1 Tbsp beaten egg white per 8-10 ozs of milk), stir and steam the mixture, covered, in boiling water for 10-15 minutes on low heat until it gels. Water should be up to 1/4 way up the bowl. Serve Egg White and Ginger Milk Pudding hot or cold. Refrigerate cold pudding. The cold pudding tastes like a delicate ginger flavored yogurt. Both variations are **Healthy and Delicious.** Ginger has potassium, magnesium, and manganese and is good for people with arthritis.

Crabmeat Fruit Salad

Fusion & Western Cuisine

Hors d'oeuvres, Hot and Cold Appetizers

Crabmeat Fruit Salad

1-2 lbs shelled crabmeat *
1 cantaloupe
1 Fuji apple, peeled
1 pear, peeled
2 white nectarines
1/2 cup blueberries or strawberries for color
1 head of green leaf lettuce, washed and spin dried
1 large crab shell, or l fresh whole lobster
3 Tbsp or more light mayonnaise, depending on how much crabmeat is used
2 Tbsp lemon juice

Peel apple, pear, and nectarines, and cut to 1/2 inch cubes; mix with lemon juice in a bowl. Scoop cantaloupe into balls and add to bowl. Mix crabmeat with mayonnaise and add half of the prepared fruit to the crabmeat. Don't over-mix as we want the crabmeat in small lumps.

Line the serving platter with lettuce. Spread the remaining half of the fruit on the lettuce and top with crabmeat fruit mixture. Place crab shell on top and garnish with "rose" made with nectarine peel. **See section on Garnish.**

I use the shell of a Pacific king crab from Australia as a garnish. If you don't want to splurge on buying a king crab, a fresh whole lobster will work equally well. Steam or boil the lobster. Place cooled whole lobster on one side of the serving platter lined with green leaf lettuce, then spread half of the fruit on top of the lettuce and top with crabmeat fruit mixture. Spread the lobster claws wide around the crabmeat mixture. Serve with lobster crackers so that guests can help themselves to the crabmeat salad and fresh lobster.

*Shelled crabmeat in a 1 lb can, by Phillips is available at Costco. Shelled crabmeat is needed to supplement the fresh shellfish as one lobster or crab does not yield enough meat for the salad. Using shelled crabmeat is the easiest way to prepare this appetizer. You can also add cooked shelled shrimp. The whole shellfish serves as a garnish as well as meat, without having the hostess do the shelling. The guests will do the work as they eat the shellfish and crabmeat salad or lobster crabmeat salad.

The crabmeat fruit salad is an **Easy and Delicious** cold appetizer for an elegant buffet or sit down dinner. Serves 10

Baked Crabmeat

3/4 lb shelled crabmeat, Phillips 1lb can (Costco)
1/2 lb frozen raw shrimp
3 slices white bread centers
1 small onion, cut in fourths
Salt, white pepper, 1/2 tsp garlic powder
2 cloves garlic, minced

2 tsp tapioca starch or cornstarch
4 Tbsp light mayonnaise
1 Tbsp pale dry sherry or Shaoxing wine
2 Tbsp minced Virginia ham
8 5-inch scallop shells, or small ramekins
Canola oil spray

Shelled and deveined shrimp are big time savers, otherwise shell and devein shrimp
with 1tsp salt while prepping; rinse in cold water and drain. Dry with paper towel to
remove excess water. Preparing shrimp with salt improves the texture of shrimp.

Trim bread crusts and soak bread centers in cold water. Squeeze out excess water in bread
center and place on paper towel to soak up remaining excess water.

Shred the Virginia ham in a food processor first, or mince by hand chopping. Set aside.
Mix the shrimp, onion, garlic, and bread in a food processor for a few seconds (by pulsing)
until you get a coarse pâte. (These ingredients can be chopped by hand until minced.)
Season and mix pâte with wine, tapioca starch, salt, white pepper, and garlic powder.
In a separate bowl, mix crabmeat with mayonnaise until moistened; season lightly with salt
and combine crabmeat and shrimp mixture.

Grease scallop shells and fill with crabmeat mixture so that it is slightly mounded.
Sprinkle crabmeat with minced Virginia ham. Spray with Canola oil.
Bake in preheated 400 degrees oven for 20-25 minutes until it's golden and slightly crusted.
Spray lightly with Canola oil and garnish with parsley. Serve hot.

This recipe makes a delicious, hot seafood appetizer that is made ahead of time and baked
when you are ready to serve dinner. **Serves 8.**
You'll love the Baked Crabmeat because it gets easier to make as you are bound to make it
again and again until it's one of your Easy and Delicious recipes. **See Mariner's Crab
cakes as a Companion Dish** for the next day if you have extra ingredients.

Hors d'oeuvres
Shrimp Toast

1/4 lb shrimp, deveined, cleaned
1 slice white bread, crust removed
1 tsp minced ham
1/2 tsp tapioca starch or cornstarch
Salt, white pepper
Garlic powder
1/2 tsp Shaoxing cooking wine or pale
dry sherry
Sweet French bread (sliced at the bakery)
Freeze extra bread in sealed plastic bag.

Moisten bread center with water first;
squeeze out extra water. Then place bread
center on paper towel to soak up remaining
excess water.
Put 1/2 tsp of salt in the shrimp while
prepping and cleaning it. Salt improves the
texture of shrimp. Rinse in cold water and
drain.
Mix the shrimp and bread in a food
processor for 30-60 seconds until the
texture is a coarse pâte; or mince by hand
chopping. Season the shrimp pâte with
garlic powder, salt, pepper, cornstarch, and
a little wine.

Place buttered and sliced French bread on
foil lined baking pan. Sprinkle with garlic
powder.   Spread a 1/4 inch layer of shrimp
pâte on bread and garnish with minced
ham. Spray with canola oil.

Bake @ 400 degrees preheated oven for
12-15 minutes. Watch that the shrimp toast
does not burn. Garnish with a leaf of
Chinese parsley, optional. Serve
immediately.

These are delicious hot hors d'oeuvres that
can be made ahead of time and baked when
ready to serve.

Traditionally, shrimp toast is a Chinese
hot hors d'oeuvre that is made with white
sliced bread and deep-fried, then cut into
triangles. But baking or broiling the shrimp
toast on sliced French bread is an easy
alternative with fewer calories. I moved
this recipe into the continental cuisine
section since I have altered the ingredients
and method of cooking, with a slightly
different taste from the original recipe.

Hors d'oeuvres
Crab Meat Dip

3/4 lb crab meat
3 Tbsp light mayonnaise
Maggi sauce
Crackers or celery sticks

Mix mayonnaise with a few dashes of
Maggi sauce to taste. Mix crabmeat with
sauce and fill a small 5-inch bowl with
the dip.

Line a compote dish or a serving bowl
with lettuce leaves and invert the dip onto
the lettuce leaves. Garnish with a sprig
of parsley. Serve with crackers or celery
sticks. If celery sticks are used, remove
celery strings first and cut celery into
2 1/2-inch lengths.

The Crabmeat Dip is a winner. It's an **Easy
and Delicious** hors d'oeuvre made in a few
minutes and kept in the refrigerator until
guests arrive.

Smoked Salmon Appetizer

French bread (sweet baguette, pre-sliced at the bakery)
Smoked Salmon, sliced
Cream cheese or Neufchatel Cream Cheese
Garlic powder
Butter or canola oil spray
Fig jam or apricot jam
Fresh dill

Butter sliced bread, or for speed and convenience,
spray with canola oil.
Sprinkle garlic powder on buttered bread.
Broil on low until lightly golden and crunchy, watching
carefully not to burn. Spread cream cheese on toasted
bread, followed by sliced smoked salmon, and jam.
Decorate with a pinch of fresh dill.
This is an **Easy and Delicious** appetizer.

Hot Appetizers

Brie en Croûte

1 package of Brie   1 puff pastry sheet
3 shitake mushrooms, diced   Crackers

Defrost 1/2 or 1/4 piece (depending on the size of the Brie) of puff pastry sheet at room temperature for 30 minutes.
Cut the Brie in half horizontally.
Microwave mushrooms for 30 seconds. Squeeze out excess water.
Sandwich the mushrooms in between the Brie halves.

Dust counter lightly with flour, and roll the puff pastry sheet to half its original thickness. Wrap the Brie and mushrooms with the pastry sheet, pinching the ends together with your fingers as if you are decorating the pastry shell of a pie. Brush the pastry sheet with egg yolk to give the pastry a glaze. You could decorate the Brie with the extra trimmings from the pastry sheet, like a mushroom or flower or whatever you want. Brush the decoration with the egg yolk also. Use a fork to pierce a few holes in the pastry wrap.

Bake in preheated oven @ 375 degrees for 15 minutes or until lightly crusted and golden. Serve hot with crackers. This is an **Easy and Delicious** hot appetizer.

Cheese Nuggets

8 ozs sharp cheddar cheese, grated
7 Tbsp unsalted butter or margarine
1/2 cup whole wheat, 1/2 cup white flour

Grate the cheddar cheese in a food processor or with a hand grater.
Leave butter at room temperature. Mix cheese with butter; add flour. Mix until blended.
Roll approximately 1/2 cup of the cheese mixture into a ball, using a plastic wrap to keep the cheese mixture together. Then shape the ball into a log by rolling it with the palm of your hand, making it approximately 6 inches long and 1 inch in diameter. By keeping the rolling all within the plastic wrap, you keep the cheese from sticking to your hands. Wrap each log with plastic wrap and freeze until ready to use.

Leave log at room temperature for 20 minutes. Cut the log into 1/3-inch thick pieces and bake in preheated oven @ 400 degrees for 10 minutes. This is a great hot appetizer that can be made well ahead of time, frozen, and baked in a few minutes. The recipe makes 3 logs for many servings. 1 log makes 8-10 nuggets. These are **Easy and Delicious** hot hors d'oeuvres.

Preparing Vietnamese Style Spring Roll

1. Preparation of Vietnamese Style Spring Roll
Layer of spinach on top of moist translucent sheet, column of chicken, mushroom & bean sprouts next to shredded roast pork, red peppers, avocado slices and roast eel (optional,) pre-washed spinach leaves.
The last 2 inches of the Spring roll sheet are left blank for sealing the roll.
Note: Plain bean sprouts can also be used without the chicken and mushrooms.

2. Preparation of Vietnamese Style Crab Roll
Layer of spinach on top of moist translucent sheet, column of green peppers next to crab meat, avocado slices, red peppers, spinach. Last 2 inches of Spring roll sheet are left blank for sealing the roll.

3. Cut Vietnamese Spring Rolls on Serving Plate

4. Vietnamese Style Spring Roll Dry Ingredients:
Vietnamese spring roll skin (round translucent sheets in package,) Vietnamese fish sauce, shredded roast pork in jar (肉鬆,) canned roasted eel, shredded roast pork in dish. Many ingredients can be substituted: smoked salmon for shredded pork and eel. Shredded roast pork can be substituted with shredded fish (魚鬆).

❤ Vietnamese Style Spring Rolls

1/2 lb bean sprouts
1/2 red bell pepper, 1/2 green bell pepper, sliced thin into 2 inch lengths
Shredded roast pork (optional ingredient, could be replaced with smoked salmon)
Roasted eel (3 1/2 oz can, optional ingredient)
1 avocado, sliced
Pre-washed baby spinach leaves or green leaf lettuce
Vietnamese Spring Roll Skin (dried translucent sheets, 8 1/2 or 9 1/2 inches in diameter)

Bean sprouts should be very fresh and not wet. Heat dry wok to high; stir and toss the bean sprouts in the dry wok on high for a few minutes to get rid of excess water in the sprouts. The sprouts are still crispy. (Or you can use the alternate method of parboiling bean sprouts in a pot of boiling water for 1 minute. Rinse in cold water, drain and spin dry). Bean sprouts will be barely cooked and very crisp. Set aside. Cut red and green peppers into long thin slices.

Soften a sheet of Spring Roll Skin in warm water (about a minute). Lift the sheet, drain water, and place on a large plate. Spread a layer of spinach leaves on the sheet, leaving the last 2 inches on the far side of the sheet unfilled, for sealing the roll.
Spread 2-3 Tbsp of bean sprouts in a column, on top of the spinach.
Add a column of shredded pork or smoked salmon next to the bean sprouts.
Add a thin column of sliced red peppers and roasted eel.
Add a thin column of sliced avocado and green peppers.
Leave the last 2 inches of the spring roll skin unfilled for sealing.

Starting on the side with the bean sprouts, carefully roll the skin into a long column. The roll is sealed with the empty portion of the Spring Roll Skin. Leave the roll with the sealed end down for 5 minutes. Cut the roll into 3 or 4 sections and place on serving platter with the flat cut ends down.
Serve with **Dipping Sauce. (See Vegetarian Hearts of Palm Rolls**)
The spring roll is quite flavorful without the dipping sauce since the shredded pork and the roasted eel add much taste to the fresh, crunchy vegetables. I serve the Spring Rolls without the sauce.

You could also make the spring rolls whenever you serve the Chicken with Mushroom and Bean Sprouts (which is an entrée). Any extras would be used as one of the main ingredients in place of the plain bean sprouts.

This is a delightfully **Healthy and Delicious** appetizer, full of fresh crunchy vegetables. It's colorful and very tantalizing. Nutritionally, the Vietnamese Style Spring Roll is chock full of vitamins and minerals and low in calories. **See Photos: Making Vietnamese Style Rolls**

Vietnamese Style Crab Rolls

The beauty of this Vietnamese Style Crab Roll is the simplicity of using raw vegetables and ingredients that require very little or no cooking at all. You can also substitute smoked salmon or other seafood for the crabmeat.

1/2 green bell pepper, sliced thin
1/2 red bell pepper, sliced thin
1/2 lb bean sprouts
2 pieces of pressed tofu, slivered
1 avocado sliced thin
1 can (3.5 oz) roasted eel
1/2 cup crab meat, mixed with 1 tsp light mayonnaise
Pre-washed spinach leaves or green leaf lettuce
Salt, oyster sauce, sugar
Vietnamese Spring Roll Skin (dried translucent sheets, 8 1/2 or 9 1/2 inches in diameter)

Parboil bean sprouts in a pot of boiling water for 1 minute. Drain well. Bean sprouts will be barely cooked and still very crisp. Sauté bean sprouts with slivered tofu and season to taste with salt, oyster sauce & sugar. Set ingredients and sliced bell peppers for wrapping.

See Photos: Making Vietnamese Style Rolls
Soak a sheet of Spring Roll Skin in warm water for about 1 minute to soften. Lift sheet, drain water and place sheet on a large plate. Spread a layer of spinach leaves on the sheet, leaving the last 2 inches on the far side of the sheet unfilled, for sealing the roll.
On top of the spinach, spread a column of bean sprouts and tofu.
Add a column of sliced green peppers next to the sprouts.
Add a column of crabmeat, followed by avocado slices, roasted eel, and sliced red peppers. Roasted eel adds a lot of flavor to the roll.

Carefully roll the filled sheet, starting on the side with the tofu and bean sprouts. Roll the sheet into a long column. Seal the roll with the unfilled portion of the sheet. Leave the roll with the sealed end down for 5 minutes. Cut the roll into thirds and place on serving platter with the flat cut ends down and the red and green peppers and avocado showing through the open-end pieces for a colorful display. If roasted eel is used, the rolls can be served without the Dipping Sauce as the roasted eel is quite flavorful. See Vegetarian Hearts of Palm Roll for **Dipping Sauce.**

This is an **Easy, Healthy and Delicious** cold appetizer. It's nutritious, low calorie, tasty, and colorful. It's loaded with vitamins A, C, & potassium.

♥ Vegetarian Hearts of Palm Rolls

1 can Hearts of Palm
Pre-washed baby spinach leaves or green leaf lettuce
1 avocado, sliced thin
1 green bell pepper, cut into long thin slices
1 red bell pepper, cut into long thin slices
Vietnamese Spring Roll Skin (dried translucent sheets, 8 1/2 or 9 1/2 inches in diameter)

See Photos: Making Vietnamese Style Rolls
Soften a sheet of Spring Roll Skin in warm water for about a minute. Lift the sheet, drain water, and place on a large plate. Spread a layer (one handful) of spinach leaves on the translucent sheet, leaving the last 2 inches on the far side of the sheet unfilled, for sealing the roll.
Place one column of hearts of palm on the spinach leaves.
Add a column of green peppers next to the hearts of palm
Add a column of sliced avocados, and a column of red bell peppers.
Leave the last 2 inches of the spring roll skin unfilled, for sealing the roll.

Carefully roll the filled skin, starting with the hearts of palm side. Roll the skin into a long column.
Seal the roll at the far side with the unfilled portion of the skin. Leave the roll with the sealed end down for 5 minutes. Cut the roll into thirds and place on a serving platter with the flat cut ends down. Serve with chilled Vietnamese Dipping Sauce.
Serves 4-6.

Dipping Sauce
3 Tbsp sugar dissolved in 3 Tbsp water
1-2 tsp Vietnamese fish sauce
1-2 tsp white distilled vinegar
1-2 tsp lime or lemon juice
1-2 cloves garlic, minced
1/4 tsp diced red bell pepper or chili pepper, seeded and diced

Combine sugar water, fish sauce, vinegar and lime or lemon juice in microwave-safe dish. Add garlic; microwave for 1 minute. Add red bell or hot pepper. Chill. The proportions for vinegar, fish sauce and peppers can be modified depending on one's individual taste for a mild or strong sauce. 4-6.

This is an **Easy, Healthy and Delicious** cold appetizer that can be whipped up in 30 minutes. It's nutritious, low calorie, tasty, and colorful. It's loaded with vitamins A, C, & potassium.

Beef Kebab

1/2 lb flank steak
1 Tbsp Lee Kum Kee double deluxe soy sauce
1 tsp oyster sauce
2 Tbsp Mirin (sweet cooking rice wine)
1 Tbsp honey

3 cloves garlic, minced
1 stalk scallion, crushed
White pepper
6 inch Bamboo skewers

Trim away the fat and white tendons from the flank steak. Cut flank steak lengthwise into 4 inch strips, then cut against the grain, and slice beef into 1/8 inch thick pieces.   Mix the above ingredients and marinate the sliced beef overnight.

Soak the skewers in water for 45 minutes first. Skewer the beef so that the meat lies flat on the skewer and broil on low for about 4-5 minutes; turn skewers over and broil 1 minute until done. Beef Kebab is an **Easy, Healthy and Delicious** appetizer served hot or cold. Serves 8-10

The inspiration for this recipe comes from our docent training at the Asian Art Museum in San Francisco. We have been studying Hindu deities. Durga is one of the Hindu goddesses created by the male gods to get rid of a nuisance buffalo demon that caused much havoc. Even the gods could not handle the problem until they created Durga. She was powerful and fearlessly used her trident, to pierce and kill the buffalo demon. I first named the recipe, Durga's Skewered Buffalo, but abandoned the name since Hindus do not eat beef even if it's skewered to perfection.

Zucchini Squares

3 cups unpeeled zucchini, sliced
1 cup Biscuit mix
1/2 cup onions, finely diced
1/2 cup grated Parmesan cheese
4 eggs, beaten

2 Tbsp parsley
1/2 tsp salt, white pepper
1/2 tsp oregano
3 cloves garlic, finely diced
1/2 cup vegetable oil

Mix all the ingredients together. Spread in greased 9 x13 Pyrex pan.
Bake in preheated 350 degrees oven for 25 minutes. Serve hot or cold.
Makes 4 dozen tasty **Easy, Healthy and Delicious** appetizers.

♥ Curried Chicken Pâte

1/2 chicken breast, cooked and diced	2 Tbsp light mayonnaise
1/2 apple, peeled and diced	1/2 tsp curry, 1/2 tsp honey
4 stalks celery hearts	Salt
1/2 cup walnuts	Crackers or celery sticks

Remove celery strings, and cut into 2 stalks of celery into 1/4 inch pieces before putting it in the food processor for a few seconds until they are cut to small pieces. Squeeze out excess water from celery. Then mix chicken breast, apples and walnuts in the food processor for a few seconds to get a coarse pâte. Combine with celery and add mayonnaise, curry, sprinkling a little at a time and season to taste with salt and honey.

Put the pâte in a small mold or a bowl which can be inverted onto a serving plate. Refrigerate. Serve with crackers or celery sticks. If celery sticks are used for dipping, cut remaining celery into 2-inch lengths.

My sister, Lily, gave me the idea for this recipe when she brought me a tray of beautifully stuffed cherry tomatoes. What a fantastic appetizer that tastes so good and looks as if it came from a caterer! I think she improvised the ingredients and said it was an easy appetizer to make. But after I played with the recipe, I figured it would be fine as a pâte, as the ingredients are simple, but not worth the time stuffing the dainty cherry tomatoes.

Shrimp on Artichoke Leaves

1 artichoke	1/8 tsp curry
1/3 lb bay shrimp	Maggi sauce
1 1/2 Tbsp light mayonnaise	Salt, white pepper

Use a medium pot to boil the artichoke until it is tender. Trim the stem of the artichoke and remove the first two layers of small outer leaves. Set aside.

Mix mayonnaise, curry (add a little at a time until you have the desired taste,) salt, pepper, a dash of Maggi sauce.
Put a small dab of the sauce on the meaty end of the artichoke leaf, with a couple of bay shrimp on top of the sauce.

Place the leaves with the shrimp in concentric circles on a large serving plate. You may need another plate for all the leaves.   Save the artichoke heart. Scoop out and throw away the fuzzy center and spread some sauce on the round artichoke heart. Put 5 or 6 bay shrimp on the sauce and make the stuffed artichoke heart the center of the platter with the leaves surrounding it. This is a cold appetizer that could be made ahead of time during the day. It looks pretty with the green leaves and pink shrimp. Serves 6-8

Coquilles St. Jacques

1 1/2 lb bay scallops or
sea scallops cut into 1/2 inch cubes
1-2 cups chicken broth
1 Tbsp pale dry sherry
1/4 cup butter or margarine
1/2 lb mushrooms, sliced
1 Tbsp lemon juice
1 onion, diced
6 Tbsp potato flour

1/2 cup whipping cream
1/8 tsp nutmeg
1 1/2 cups (about 1/2 lb) Swiss cheese, shredded
1/4 cup parsley
1/2 of 3 oz packet roasted garlic mashed potato
or 1 fresh mashed potato, seasoned
1/2 cup whole milk
Six 5-inch scallop shells

Coquilles St. Jacques is a luscious scallop entrée with melted cheese and mushrooms that will elicit many encores. The beauty of this hot entrée is that it could be made ahead of time and baked whenever you are ready to serve dinner.

Prepare Roasted Garlic Mashed Potatoes according to package directions or make your own mashed potato and season with garlic spread and salt. Lightly grease the scallop shells and spread with a very thin layer of mashed potatoes.

Cook scallops in 1 cup boiling chicken broth and wine for 3-4 minutes on medium heat until scallops are barely cooked. Do not overcook scallops. Let cool and drain juice. Add enough chicken broth to make 2 cups of scallop juice. Set aside scallops, and refrigerate.

Sauté mushrooms in 2 Tbsp of butter with lemon juice; cook on medium until juice evaporates. Set aside. Sauté onions in 2 Tbsp of butter until softened. Add flour; cook and stir. Gradually add scallop juice stirring with a wire whisk, and cook until thick and creamy.
Add cream, nutmeg, 1/2 cup of cheese and mushrooms; mix and cook on low for 3-5 min.

When sauce is cooled, add scallops, parsley, and season with salt and pepper.
Fill the shells with scallop and mushroom mixture. Sprinkle cheese on top.
Cover and refrigerate. Leave at room temperature for 45 minutes before baking. Bake in preheated oven @400 degrees until bubbly and cheese is lightly brown (12-14 minutes.)
Extra filling could be saved and baked the following day with equally fine results.

Everyone will love this gourmet hot and scrumptious appetizer or seafood entrée. Serves 6

Filet Mignon with Chestnuts en Croûte

Fusion & Western Entrées

Filet Mignon with Chestnuts en Croûte
Medallion Chicken with Jewelled Rice
en Croûte
Medallion Chicken with Chestnuts en Croûte
Salmon en Croûte
Bouchée à la Reine
Mariner's Crab Cakes
Salmon with Fuji Apples & Shitake Mushrooms
Debbie's Crabmeat Quiche
Stuffed Halibut with Shrimp and Crab Meat

Beef Brisket
Florentine Chicken
Shellfish with Fragrant Rice
Vegetarian Fragrant Rice
Stuffed Prawns with Crab Meat
Sesame Encrusted Ahi Tuna
Sesame Encrusted Ahi Tuna with Shitake
Mushroom Sauce
Roast Pork Loin with Red Onions

Filet Mignon with Chestnuts en Croûte

If you like Beef Wellington, you will love the Filet Mignon with Chestnuts en Croûte, which is made with chestnut pâte instead of pâte de foie gras. I find the goose liver pâte too rich. **This is a leaner version of a gourmet entrée that is delicious and gorgeous.**

4 small 6-oz filet mignons
15 fresh shitake mushrooms
5 ozs peeled and roasted chestnuts
1 sheet frozen puff pastry
1/2 small yellow onion (1 cup diced)
3 cloves garlic, minced
1 cup chicken broth

2 Tbsp cooking wine
1 tsp double deluxe soy sauce
2 tsp oyster sauce
Salt, white pepper, garlic spread
3-4 tsp sugar
1 Tbsp olive, peanut, or corn oil
1/2 egg yolk

Buy ready to eat shelled and peeled chestnuts, found in Chinese super markets. If this variety is not available, then buy frozen chestnuts and cook in chicken broth until tender. If chestnuts are unavailable, bake filets with onions and mushrooms.

Defrost pastry sheet for 40 minutes. Wash mushrooms and remove stems. Trim fat and white membranes from the filet mignons. Season filets with soy sauce, and white pepper. In a heavy nonstick pan, quickly sear both sides of filets on high heat. Remove from pan, and season lightly with garlic spread. In same pan, sauté diced onions and garlic in oil until onions are cooked. Add whole mushrooms, 1 cup of chicken broth, wine, oyster sauce and sugar; sauté and cook on medium with covered lid for 10-15 minutes until mushrooms are tender and all the juice is absorbed. Sugar is added to remove the bitterness in shitake mushrooms. Season to taste; sample mushroom, and add more sugar if needed. Set aside whole mushrooms. In food processor, pulse chestnuts with cooked onions and 2 Tbsp of chicken broth for 5-6 seconds until you get a coarse dry pâte. Form pâte into 4 thin patties.

Dust both sides of pastry sheet with flour and roll it out to a large thin rectangle big enough to wrap all the filets.
Cut into 4 rectangles. Place a filet on one side of a pastry rectangle. Put chestnut pâte on top of the beef and top with 3-4 shitake mushrooms. Fold pastry sheet over the top and pinch the edges together on all three sides so that the entire filet is wrapped. Wrap the other three filets the same way. Brush egg yolk on pastry sheet. Cut thin slivers of pastry sheet from trimmings into 1/16th inch strips and place them in a crisscross pattern on top of the wrapped filets, as in a lattice pie crust. Lightly brush the pastry strips with egg yolk. Bake in a preheated oven @ 400 degrees for 15-20 minutes until pastry has a light brown crust. Ovens vary, and depending on the thickness of the filets, the baking time will vary. Serve with a tossed salad and green vegetable.

The filet mignon is tender and medium rare. **It is a dazzling gourmet entrée that looks beautiful and has the delectable taste of succulent beef with chestnut pâte and shitake mushrooms that melt in your mouth. See Photo on p. 117.**

Making Medallion Chicken

1. One chicken filet with rice stuffing folded over and one chicken filet with rice stuffing that is open, ready to be folded.
2. Two rolled chicken filets with rice stuffing, connected in the middle with extra rice stuffing, placed on top of rolled pastry sheet.
3. Chicken filets with rice stuffing & rolled pastry sheet slit and partially wrapped.
4. Chicken filet wrapped with pastry sheet & brushed with egg yolk.
5. Baked and cut Medallion Chicken with Jeweled Rice.
6. Baked and cut Medallion Chicken with Chestnuts wrapped the same way.

Medallion Chicken
with Jeweled Rice en Croûte

1 chicken breast filet, cut to 2 half filets
1 1/2 cups sweet or glutinous rice
1 puff pastry sheet, defrosted 40 minutes
6 dried black mushrooms, presoaked 4 hrs
1 link pork sausage, steamed 35 minutes, diced
2 Tbsp small dried shrimp, 2 Tbsp diced Virginia ham
3 cloves minced garlic, chicken broth, 1 egg yolk, 1Tbsp oil
1 Tbsp oyster sauce, 1 tsp soy sauce, pepper, garlic powder
4 Tbsp pine nuts, toasted in oven for 15 min @230 degrees
Chicken marinade: Mix 1 Tbsp light mayonnaise, 1 tsp mustard, 1 tsp honey

Cook rice in the rice cooker using chicken broth instead of water, using 4 Tbsp less liquid than usual. Remove stems of mushrooms. Use a Teflon pan to sauté diced mushrooms and garlic in 1Tbsp hot oil; add dried shrimp, diced ham, sausage, and cook for 5 min. Add cooked sweet rice, pine nuts, soy sauce, and oyster sauce. Mix well and set aside.

Trim white tendons in breast filets. For ease of handling, butterfly chicken breast filets when they are **half defrosted** by cutting filet horizontally, leaving one long edge attached. Choose the straightest and thickest portion of the filet to be uncut. The cut breast filet is half the original thickness and twice its width; the halves unfold like a butterfly. Dry with paper towel if wet. Season cut filets with salt, pepper, and chicken marinade mix.

Put a layer of rice (1/3 +) on the chicken filet. Carefully fold the left side of the chicken filet with layered rice towards the middle, and fold the right side portion over the left side into a **rolled chicken filet** (with rice layered in the middle.) The center portion of the filet does not move; only the two sides of the filet are folded towards the center. It's okay if the roll is not perfect since the pastry hides the imperfections. Follow the same procedure to roll the second chicken filet. **See Photos: Making Medallion Chicken.**

Dust the puffed pastry sheet on both sides with flour and roll it out to a 12" x 16" rectangle that will wrap the 2 rolled chicken breast filets. Transfer pastry to a large sheet of aluminum foil on a cookie sheet. Place the filets in a column on the pastry sheet. Use the remaining rice to connect the two rolled filets in the middle. Cut 3/4 inch wide strips on the pastry sheet on both sides of the chicken roll filets. Then take the pastry strips and wrap them over the chicken and rice roll. The puff pastry strips will overlap on top of the rolled filets. Seal the two ends by pinching the dough together and trim extra dough. Brush egg yolk on the pastry.

Bake in a 400 degree preheated oven for 25 -28 minutes or until the pastry is lightly golden and crusted. Serve the Medallion Chicken with Jeweled Rice, with lots of fresh parsley and cherry tomatoes surrounding the roll. It's a **beautiful gourmet entrée** for 10. The recipe could be halved using a 1/2 breast filet.

❤ Medallion Chicken with Chestnuts en Croûte

1 large half chicken breast filet
8 oz chestnuts, shelled and peeled
1/4 cup dried cranberries, fresh parsley
1 cup white mushrooms, thinly sliced
1 cup chicken broth
Salt, pepper, garlic powder
Marinade:1 tsp light mayonnaise, 1/2 tsp Dijon mustard, 1/2 tsp honey
1/2 sheet of frozen puff pastry, defrosted to room temperature; egg yolk for glazing

Trim white tendons in breast filet. For ease of handling, butterfly the filet when it is **half defrosted** by cutting the filet horizontally, leaving one long edge attached. Choose the straightest and thickest portion of the filet to be uncut. The cut filet is half the original thickness and twice its width; the halves unfold like a butterfly. Dry with paper towel if wet. Season cut filet with salt, pepper, garlic powder, mayonnaise, mustard and honey.

Buy the shelled, peeled, and ready to eat chestnuts found in Chinese supermarkets. If those are not available, buy frozen chestnuts and cook in chicken broth on low for 20-30 minutes until very tender. Leave 8 chestnuts whole for garnish. Sauté mushrooms in 1/2 Tbsp oil until water from the mushroom is evaporated. Mix 2 Tbsp mushrooms with chestnuts in food processor for 3 seconds until crumbly. Add remaining mushrooms and cranberries to the mixture and set aside.

Put a layer of chestnuts, cranberries and mushrooms on the chicken filet. Fold left side of filet to the center, then fold right side over the left so that it looks like a roll with chestnut filling inside the chicken filet. It's okay if the roll is not perfect since the pastry hides the imperfections. **See Photos of Medallion Chicken with Jeweled Rice en Croûte** with two rolled filets connected in the middle. The same wrap technique is used for one filet.

Dust the puff pastry sheet on both sides with flour; roll it out to a rectangle that will wrap the rolled chicken breast filet. Transfer to a large piece of aluminum foil on a cookie sheet. Place the rolled chicken filet in the middle of the pastry sheet. Cut 3/4-inch wide strips on the pastry sheet on both sides of the chicken. Then take the pastry strips and wrap over the chicken. The puff pastry strips will overlap on top of the rolled chicken. Trim extra dough; seal up the two ends by pinching the dough together. Brush egg yolk on the pastry. Recipe can be doubled. See Medallion Chicken with Jeweled Rice.

Bake in a 400 degrees preheated oven for 20 minutes or until the pastry is lightly golden and crusted. Turn off the oven and let it sit in the oven for another 5 minutes. Serve Medallion Chicken garnished with whole chestnuts and lots of fresh parsley. The **Gourmet Medallion Chicken looks beautiful encrusted with a golden pastry and a swirl of chestnuts in the middle as you slice it.** Serves 4.

♥ Salmon En Croûte

1 thick salmon filet (2-3lbs)
1 lb prewashed spinach
2 cups mushrooms, sliced
1 frozen puff pastry sheet
1 Tbsp oil
2 oz. butter or margarine
1/2 tsp lemon or lime juice

Salt, white pepper, garlic powder
1 Tbsp light mayonnaise
1 tsp mustard
1 tsp honey
1 egg yolk
2 tsp herbes de Provence or
Fresh dill and thyme

Sauce: Melt 2 Tbsp of butter and whisk in 2 Tbsp of potato flour over low heat. Whisk 3/4 cup milk, adding a little bit first until sauce is smooth, then gradually whisk the rest with 3/4 cup chicken broth. Bring to a boil and season with salt and white pepper.

Cut salmon lengthwise into two long pieces. Season salmon with salt, pepper, garlic powder, and herbes de Provence. Mix mayonnaise, mustard, and honey in a bowl and spread 2/3 of mixture on all four sides of salmon filet. Keep cut salmon in its original shape.

Divide the spinach in half and microwave 1 minute for each portion until the leaves are limp. Cool. Squeeze out excess water. Mix spinach with 1 tsp of oil and the remaining 1/3 of the honey mustard mixture in a food processor for a split second. Set aside.
Sauté sliced mushrooms in butter, add lemon juice, salt, garlic powder. Set aside.

Defrost puff pastry sheet at room temperature for 40 minutes. Dust pastry sheet with flour on both sides, and roll into a rectangular shape that is 2 inches longer than the salmon in length, and 21/4 times the width of the fish so that it could wrap the salmon. (Pastry sheet can be lengthened by attaching strips into a longer piece if needed for wrap.) Transfer the pastry sheet onto a large piece of greased heavy aluminum foil placed on a broiler pan or long cookie sheet.

Place bottom half of salmon filet in the middle of pastry sheet. Put a layer of spinach on top of salmon, then a layer of mushrooms, then salmon. Make sure that salmon is stacked in its original shape with matching ends. Top with either fresh dill and thyme or a sprinkling of Herbes de Provence. Cut 1/2 inch slits on the pastry sheet on both sides of the salmon. Fold slit pastry strips over the salmon from both sides and attach slit pastry strips on top of the salmon, sealing up the entire salmon down the middle from end to end.

Brush egg yolk over the pastry sheet. Bake in preheated oven @ 400 for 25 minutes until it has a golden crust. Serve with sauce. Wait 30 minutes before cutting the salmon into serving pieces. See Photo of Medallion Chicken re: wrapping.

This is my sister, Lily's gourmet signature dish. I made some modifications to her original recipe. It's a dazzling entrée for company. Serves 10-12

Bouchée à la Reine

1 package of frozen puff pastry shells
1 whole chicken breast filet cut to 1/2" pieces
1 lb white mushrooms, sliced
3 hard boiled eggs, diced
5 slices lean bacon
Vegetable oil
5 cloves garlic, minced
Pale dry sherry

Sauce:
2 Tbsp butter
2 Tbsp potato flour
1 cup whole milk or
1 cup soy milk
1 cup chicken broth
Salt, pepper

Sauce: Melt 2 Tbsp butter; mix with 2 Tbsp potato flour over low heat. Whisk 1 cup of whole or soy milk into the mixture, putting in a little first until sauce is smooth, then add the rest. Whisk over medium heat. Add 1 cup of chicken broth, salt, pepper. Add more potato flour if you want a thick sauce.

Bake puff pastry shells in preheated oven @ 400 degrees for 20-25 minutes. Carve out the cap of the patty shells and set aside.
Sauté sliced mushrooms in oil, with a sprinkle of lemon juice. Set aside.
Microwave bacon between double layers of paper towel to get rid of the fat. Crumble the crisp bacon into bits and set aside.

Sauté chicken with minced garlic in 2 Tbsp oil; add wine, and cook on medium until chicken is barely cooked. Add sauce and simmer for about 10 minutes.
Add mushroom, bacon, and eggs to chicken and bring the contents to a low boil.
Put baked shells on individual serving plates, and pour chicken and mushrooms over the shells. Top with the cap of the shell.

Variation: Shrimp or scallops can be used in place of chicken breast. Reduce cooking time if shellfish is used.

This is an entrée that I modified based on an old recipe from a friend who claimed Bouchée à la Reine has "morsels fit for a queen."

Mariner's Crab Cakes

3/4 lb shelled crabmeat (1lb. can or fresh crabmeat)
1/2 lb shrimp, minced
3 slices white bread, crusts removed
5 thin slices of Virginia ham, (1/8 cup, minced in food processor seperately)
1 onion, minced
Salt, white pepper
2 cloves garlic, minced
2 tsp tapioca starch or cornstarch
1/2 tsp garlic powder
4 Tbsp light mayonnaise
1 tsp pale dry sherry or Shaoxing wine
3 Tbsp vegetable oil
Mint leaves for garnish

Sauce: Mix 2 Tbsp light mayonnaise, 1tsp wasabi, 1/2 tsp honey

Shell and devein the shrimp with 1tsp of salt while prepping, rinse in cold water and drain. Salt improves the texture of shrimp.
Soak the bread for a few minutes in cold water. Squeeze out excess water. Use paper towel to soak up excess water after squeezing.

Mix the shrimp, half of the minced ham, onion, garlic, and bread in a food processor for 30 seconds into a coarse pâte. (These ingredients can also be chopped by hand until minced.) Season shrimp mixture with wine, tapioca starch, salt, white pepper, and garlic powder. Mix ingredients well. In a separate bowl, mix crabmeat with mayonnaise until moistened; season lightly with salt. Combine crabmeat and shrimp mixture.

Use two large spoons to make 12 round balls, about the size of golf balls. Refrigerate covered. When ready to serve, heat 2 Tbsp of oil in a non-stick pan; flatten the balls slightly with a spatula and lightly brown the crab cakes on each side with the pan covered, turning the cakes over several times so that they don't get too brown. Cook on medium for about 8-10 minutes until done.
Serves 6 (two crab cakes per serving)
Garnish crab cakes with mint leaf. Serve with a dab of sauce.
The crab cakes are actually quite easy to make using a food processor. They make a delicious seafood appetizer for 12 or a delectable lunch entrée for 6 with bread and a fresh salad.

See **Baked Crabmeat** for variations on the same theme using similar ingredients with totally different presentations as hot appetizers.

124

♥ Salmon with Fuji Apples & Shitake Mushrooms

2 1bs Salmon filet, skin removed
2 large Fuji apples
1 lb fresh shitake mushrooms
4 cups of broccoli florets
6 cloves garlic, minced
Salt, white pepper, sugar
2 tsp Lee Kum Kee double deluxe soy sauce
or light soy sauce

1 Tbsp oyster sauce
1 1/2 cup chicken broth
2 pieces of raw sugar (about 2 Tbsp)
1 Tbsp white wine, 2 tsp tapioca starch
or cornstarch
1 Tbsp vegetable oil
Canola oil spray

Fish marinade: Mix 2 tsp light mayonnaise, 1 tsp mustard, 1/2 tsp honey

Rinse salmon in cold water and dry with paper towel. Season salmon filet with salt, white pepper, and fish marinade. Peel and cut apples in half; core and slice into 1/4 inches. Spread sliced apples on foil and spray with Canola oil and sprinkle with sugar before sealing the aluminum foil. Bake apple slices in a preheated oven @ 350 degrees for about 15 minutes until apples are softened.

Sautée minced garlic in oil for 3 minutes until lightly brown. Add fresh shitake mushrooms with stems removed, soy sauce, oyster sauce, chicken broth, raw sugar and wine. Cook on medium heat for 10-15 minutes until mushrooms are ready. Mix 2 tsp of tapioca starch with 2 Tbsp of sauce and whisk in to thicken sauce over medium heat. On a large piece of heavy foil, coat 2 Tbsp of mushroom sauce on both sides of salmon and arrange baked sliced apples in 2 rows on top of fish. Seal the salmon with foil and bake in a preheated oven @ 375 degrees for about 12-18 minutes until salmon is done. Pour hot mushroom sauce on Salmon with fresh shitake mushrooms surrounding the fish. Garnish with cooked broccoli florets or parsley. (Small individual cuts of salmon filet can be cooked directly in the mushroom sauce instead of being baked.) Serves 8 or more. This is an **Easy, Healthy and Delicious seafood entrée.**

Debbie's Crabmeat Quiche

8 ozs crabmeat
1 cup sliced Swiss or Monterey Jack
2 slices crisp bacon, crumbled
1 green onion, chopped

3 eggs
1 cup whipping cream
Salt, white pepper
1 frozen deep dish pie crust

Use a fork to pierce some holes on the sides and bottom of the pie crust. Line pie crust with cheese.
Mix eggs and cream well. Add bacon crumbs and scallions, and season to taste with seasoned salt and pepper. Pour mixture into pie crust.

Bake in preheated 375 degree oven for 40 minutes until filling is set and crust is golden.
6 servings. This is an **Easy and Delicious** crabmeat quiche.

Stuffed Halibut with Shrimp and Crab Meat

1 1/2 lb Halibut filet
1/3 lb frozen raw shrimp
1/3 lb crab meat
1 slice of white bread
2 Tbsp light mayonnaise
2 tsp mustard
1 tsp honey
Salt, white pepper

Garlic powder
Paprika
1/2 cup whole milk
1-2 tsp potato flour
1 Tbsp wine
Sesame oil
Canola oil (optional)
1 lemon, cut into wedges

Buy shelled and deveined raw shrimp to save time in preparation. Sprinkle 1/2 tsp salt on shrimp while preparing and cutting it lengthwise and then into 1/2 inch pieces. Rinse shrimp in cold water to get rid of salt and drain. Dry with paper towel. Salt improves the texture of shrimp. Trim crusts from bread and soak bread center in water, then squeeze out excess water. Put bread center on paper towel to soak up excess water after squeezing.

Cut fish into 4 servings and slit half way through lengthwise each fish filet for stuffing. Season fish filet with salt, pepper, wine, and garlic powder.
Mix mayonnaise, mustard and honey to make the sauce. Use 2 Tbsp of sauce to mix with the shrimp and bread; then add crab meat to the mixture. Spread remaining sauce on the fish filet before stuffing the slit center with the shrimp and crab meat mixture so that the center is slightly mounded. Sprinkle stuffed halibut with a dash of paprika and garlic powder. Place stuffed fish filet on a large sheet of heavy aluminum foil and seal all sides so that the juice is retained inside the foil wrap.

Bake in preheated 350 degrees oven for 15-20 minutes. When fish is done, open the aluminum foil and pour out the fish juice into a small pan and heat over medium heat. Mix 1-2 tsp of potato flour with 1/2 cup of whole milk and whisk the mixture into the fish juice over medium heat to make the fish sauce. Season with a dash of sesame oil. Broil the stuffed halibut on low for a few minutes or until the top is slightly crusted. Spray lightly with canola oil. (optional) Serve with rice, sauce, a wedge of fresh lemon, and Fresh Roasted Vegetables. (See Recipe) The Stuffed Halibut is tender and juicy, a terrific **Easy and Delicious** seafood entrée. Serves 4

Beef Brisket

1 fresh beef brisket, 3-4 lbs
1 oz Lipton dry onion dip mix (1 envelope)
Heavy aluminum Foil

Take a sheet of heavy aluminum foil that is 1 1/2 times larger than the brisket.
Place the brisket in the middle of the foil. Sprinkle half of the onion dip mix on the bottom of the brisket, and the remainder on top.
Fold the aluminum foil carefully sealing the top and side edges. By folding it twice, steam does not leak out. Use a second layer of foil and place the wrapped brisket on top. Rewrap the brisket the same way, without turning it over. The meat will be tender with lots of juice or gravy if the wrap is carefully done. Wrap the brisket as if you are wrapping a package.

Bake @ 325 degrees for 3 hrs. Serves 6-8 depending on the size of the brisket.
Beef Brisket is a delicious and substantial entrée for a ski weekend at the condo. Brisket can be baked and frozen ahead of time, defrosted during the day, baked and reheated in its original foil wrap. Serve with baked yams and a tossed salad. The Beef Brisket is an **Easy and Delicious** entrée.

♥ Florentine Chicken

12-15 chicken drumsticks, skin removed
.7oz packet (16 grams) of dried Italian dressing
1 package spinach fettuccine
1/4 cup vegetable oil

1/4 cup wine vinegar
2 Tbsp mustard
1 Tbsp honey
1/2 cup water

Cook spinach fettuccine according to package instructions. Drain and place in an oven safe serving dish.

On a large sheet of heavy aluminum foil, mix chicken drumsticks with the Italian dressing, wine vinegar, water, mustard, and honey.

Bake in a preheated oven @ 350 degrees for 35-45 minutes until chicken is lightly glazed. During the last 10 minutes of baking, mix some of the sauce with fettuccine, then arrange drumsticks on top of pasta and brush meat with remaining juice. Serve with a tossed salad. Florentine Chicken is an **Easy, Healthy and Delicious entrée.**

Shellfish with Fragrant Rice

3 cups long grain rice
6-7 cups chicken broth*
7-8 Tbsp canned tomato soup,
low sodium
4 Tbsp olive oil
2 Tbsp white cooking wine
12 large prawns with heads and shells
12 medium size shrimp, shelled and
deveined
12 clams
12 mussels, optional

12 scallops
1/2 lb bay scallops
3 3/4 ozs can smoked oysters, optional
1 onion, diced into 1/2 inch pieces
3 cloves of garlic, minced
1 Tbsp tapioca starch or
1Tbsp corn starch
2 tsp garlic powder
2 tsp saffron, crumbled

Use the measuring cup that comes with the electric rice cooker (equivalent to 3/4 cup standard measuring cup) to measure the rice. Use chicken broth instead of water in the exact proportion as you would ordinarily in an electric rice cooker, less 5 Tbsp of chicken broth plus 2 Tbsp of olive oil, and 3 Tbsp canned tomato soup. Start rice cooker.

Scrub the shells of mussels and clams with a hard brush. Rinse and soak in cold water with a few drops of oil. Leave the heads and shells of the large prawns intact. Devein prawns and shrimp and prep with 1/2 tsp salt while cleaning the shrimp. Rinse in cold water, drain and place on paper towel. Salt improves the texture of prawns and shrimp. Mix 1 Tbsp corn starch with shelled shrimp and scallops. Set aside.

Bring 5cups of chicken broth to a boil; then add clams and mussels in separate batches and cook on medium heat. Remove shells immediately from boiling broth as they open; some shells take longer to open. Use a coffee filter or paper towel to filter juice from the clams and mussels to get rid of any sand. Save juice for broth.

Sauté 2 Tbsp olive oil with minced garlic, garlic powder, saffron and onions. Add 2 cups of broth, 4-5 Tbsp of tomato soup and wine, and cook 8-12 minutes until onions are soft. Add prawns, shrimp and scallops and sauté for 5-6 minutes until the shellfish is cooked. Season to taste. It's cooked when the shrimp turns pink. Do not overcook shellfish. Add cooked clams, mussels, and smoked oysters to the sauce.

Put rice in a large serving dish and pour shellfish on top. Mix rice slightly with the seafood, leaving clams and mussels and prawns on top. Cook more rice if you are serving more people. Serves 6-8. Shellfish with Fragrant Rice is a delicious entrée that can be made with a variety of fresh seafood that is available at your local seafood market.

* Chicken broth can be substituted with Mushroom Seasoning for vegetarians. Use 1 tsp of mushroom seasoning with 1cup of water for 1 cup of chicken broth. **See photo of Ingredients for mushroom seasoning on p. 17.**

♥ Vegetarian Fragrant Rice

2 cups long grain rice
3-4 cups chicken broth*
1 rutabaga, peeled and sliced into 1/8 inch pieces
1 small red yam (Beauregard yam)
peeled and sliced into 1/8 inch pieces
1/2 cup baby carrots
2 zucchinis, sliced
1/2 cup white mushrooms, halved
1 small onion, cut into 1 inch pieces
1 green bell pepper, cut into eighths
1 red bell pepper cut into eighths

6 Tbsp canned tomato soup, low sodium
4 Tbsp olive oil
1-2 tsp Balsamic vinegar
1 Tbsp honey
2 tsp garlic spread or powder
Salt, white pepper
2 tsp herbes de Provence or
Italian seasoning
1-2 tsp saffron, crumbled
2 tsp potato flour

This dish appeals to vegetarians who may add or delete vegetables to suit individual taste. Use the measuring cup that comes with the electric rice cooker (equivalent to 3/4 cup standard measuring cup) to measure the rice. Use chicken broth instead of water in the exact proportion as you would ordinarily in an electric rice cooker, less 5 Tbsp of chicken broth plus 1 Tbsp of olive oil, and 3 Tbsp canned tomato soup. Start rice cooker.

Mix 3 Tbsp olive oil, Herbes de Provence and garlic powder or garlic spread with cut vegetables. Sprinkle crumbled saffron on the vegetables and bake sliced rutabaga, yam, and baby carrots in preheated oven @ 375 degrees for 10 minutes.
Mix Balsamic vinegar with honey first and then toss with the all the roasted and remaining vegetables. Continue roasting @ 375 degrees for 10-15 minutes; roast mushrooms during the last 5 minutes, until the vegetables are done. Season to taste.

A dry wok is very convenient for tossing and mixing the oil and seasoning with a large amount of vegetables.

Toss roasted vegetables and spread on top of rice in a 3 inch deep serving dish. Heat 1 1/2 cups of chicken broth and 3 Tbsp of tomato soup to a boil; Mix 2 tsp of potato flour with 2 Tbsp of chicken broth and whisk into hot broth. Pour broth over vegetables and rice. **The Vegetarian Fragrant Rice** is chock full of vitamin A, potassium, and magnesium. Serves 4-6. **See Photo of Vegetarian Fragrant Rice on opposite page.**

* Chicken broth can be substituted with Mushroom Seasoning for vegetarians. Use 1 tsp of mushroom seasoning with 1 cup of water for 1 cup of chicken broth. **See Photo of Ingredients.**

Stuffed Prawns with Crab Meat P. 132

Stuffed Prawns with Crab Meat

12 large prawns with tail, over 1/2 lb
2 1/2 cups or 1 lb of crab meat
5 slices white bread, crust removed
3 Tbsp light mayonnaise
2 tsp mustard
2 tsp honey
Salt, white pepper, paprika
Garlic powder

Johnny's Garlic Spread Seasoning
2 cloves garlic, minced
2 red yams, (Beauregard yam) peeled
1 Tbsp olive oil & dash of Herbes de
Provence, or Italian seasoning
Canola oil spray
Mint leaf for garnish

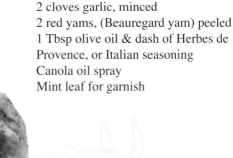

Leave the shell on the tail end of prawns. Prepare prawns with 1/2 tsp salt while shelling and deveining the prawns. Salt improves the texture of prawns. Rinse in cold water and drain; dry with paper towel. Or buy shelled and deveined prawns with the shell on the tail ends. Cut half way through the prawns where the deveining took place so that the prawn will sit flat along the cut edge. A clean cut makes the prawn sit beautifully with the tail flipped upward when stuffed with crabmeat. Season prawns with white pepper, garlic powder, Garlic Spread Seasoning, and refrigerate.

Soak bread center with water; squeeze out water and then place on paper towel to remove excess liquid. Mix mayonnaise, mustard, honey, salt, pepper, garlic powder, and a dash of Garlic Spread Seasoning. Coat prawns with 2 tsp of sauce. Stir remaining sauce with the bread center until it is well mixed; then add crab meat. Do not over mix because we want some of the crab meat in small lumps. Add more sauce to the crab meat mixture if needed to achieve a consistency that is just moist enough to make 12 balls (golf ball size) of crab meat. Set the crabmeat balls on the seasoned prawns and fold the tail over the ball so that the tail wraps around the ball and the tail end split like a rabbit's ears. The stuffed prawns look like bunny rabbits. **See Photo.**

Peel 2 yams and cut into twelve diagonal 1/4 inch slices. Coat yam slices with olive oil and a dash of Herbes de Provence or Italian seasoning and bake on a foil lined pan for 15 minutes in a preheated oven @375 degrees. Cool.

Set a stuffed prawn on a slice of cooled baked yam. Sprinkle a dash of paprika for color. Arrange stuffed prawns on a baking sheet, covered with plastic wrap, and keep refrigerated until ready to bake. Leave stuffed prawns at room temperature for 40 minutes and spray with canola oil just before baking in a preheated oven for 8-10 minutes @ 375 degrees until it is lightly crusted. Watch the prawns during the last 5 minutes and do not let it get too crusty. Garnish with a sprig of mint or parsley. Serve stuffed prawns with whole yam or baked potato, and a green vegetable or salad. Serves 4 or more. The Stuffed Prawns with Crabmeat is a **glamorous gourmet** dish.

Sesame Encrusted Ahi Tuna

133

❤ Sesame Encrusted Ahi Tuna

3/4 lb fresh Ahi tuna sashimi
3/4 cup white sesame seeds
1/8 tsp black sesame seeds, optional
Salt, white pepper, 1 tsp sugar
1 Tbsp LKK double deluxe soy sauce
1-2 Tbsp oil, Wasabi

Buy very fresh tuna filet that is the quality of sashimi. Go to a market that sells sashimi and look for tuna sashimi (not tuna steak,) with practically no visible white sheaths that separate the meat. The key to the success of this gourmet dish is to choose the cut very carefully in order to find the tenderest filet which means the cut with the least visible white sheaths. Time the shopping for the fish so that you don't keep the tuna more than a day or two in the refrigerator.

Mix soy sauce with sugar in a small side dish and wasabi in a separate dish. The sauces can be mixed by the guests according to each individual preference for a sharp or mild wasabi sauce.

Toast black and white sesame seeds in a dry skillet or Teflon pan over medium heat for about 10 minutes while shaking the pan. Do not burn the seeds. Let the seeds cool completely. Rinse tuna in cold water and dry with paper towel. Sprinkle salt and white pepper on tuna sashimi and coat with cooled, toasted sesame seeds on all sides.

Sear tuna filets in a Teflon pan with 1 Tbsp oil on medium heat for 10 seconds on each side until the tuna is barely done on the crust, but completely rare in the center. Remove from pan. Ahi tuna is very tender when served rare, still red in the middle. If the center turns white, the tuna filet will be dry and overdone. Use a sharp knife to cut tuna filet into 1/4 inch slices and place immediately on cooled serving plate with garnish. Cover with plastic wrap and refrigerate.

The tuna melts in your mouth and makes a fantastic seafood entrée. A small cut weighing about 3-4ozs can be prepared the same way, cut into 1/4 inch slices with a sharp knife, and served cold with a tossed salad as a gourmet appetizer. The Ahi tuna can also be sliced thin and served on triangular corn chips and topped with a dab of avocado and a sprig of fresh dill. The finger food Ahi Tuna appetizer is combined with the corn chip just before serving to ensure a crusty chip with yummy tuna sashimi. **The Sesame Encrusted Ahi Tuna is an Easy and Delicious gourmet treat.**

♥ Sesame Encrusted Ahi Tuna with Shitake Mushroom Sauce

1/2 lb fresh Ahi Tuna sashimi
1/2 cup white sesame seeds
1/8 tsp black sesame seeds, optional
Salt, white pepper
Dash of garlic powder
1-2 Tbsp oil
Additional ingredients:
5 fresh shitake mushrooms, stems removed

1/4 yellow onion, diced
11/2 cup chicken broth
Dash of LKK double deluxe soy sauce
Dash of LKK dark mushroom sauce for color
Oyster sauce
Salt, white pepper, garlic powder
1 tsp raw sugar

The Sesame Encrusted Ahi Tuna with Shitake Mushroom Sauce is a variation of the Sesame Encrusted Ahi Tuna that follows the same preparation steps up until the Ahi tuna is sliced. Sautée 5 fresh shitake mushrooms and 1/4 onion in 1Tbsp of olive oil. Add 11/2 cups chicken broth, a dash of LKK double deluxe soy sauce, salt, pepper, garlic powder and cook on low, covered, for about 20 minutes until mushrooms and onions are tender. Then purée the cooked mushrooms and onions in a blender until ingredients are smooth and velvety. Cook the mushroom sauce for a minute and season to taste with a dash of oyster sauce, 1 tsp of raw sugar, and a dash of LKK dark mushroom sauce for color. Serve hot shitake mushroom sauce in a separate gravy bowl with sliced Sesame Encrusted Ahi Tuna. This is an **Easy and Healthy hot gourmet appetizer.**

Roast Pork Loin with Sweet Red Onions

1 fresh pork loin (4 lbs)
4 large sweet red onions
2 1/2 cups red wine
3 Tbsp Lee Kum Kee double deluxe soy sauce or light soy sauce
1 Tbsp dark soy sauce
2 pieces of rock sugar (about 2 Tbsp raw sugar)
2 star anise
1 Tbsp vegetable oil
Pork Marinade: 6 cloves of minced garlic, 2 Tbsp Dijon mustard, 1 Tbsp double deluxe soy sauce, salt, white pepper, garlic powder, 1 Tbsp peppercorn, 1 Tbsp red wine, 1Tbsp oil, 1 tsp honey

Marinate the pork loin overnight using the pork marinade. If you buy a fresh pork loin that is seasoned, then you do not need to marinate the meat overnight as it is already prepared.

Peel and cut red onions in half, then slice into 1/4 inch pieces. Sautée onions in hot oil for 5 minutes; add 1/4 cup of wine, l Tbsp of double deluxe soy sauces, and star anise to onions. Spread onion on foil-lined broiler pan and then set pork roast, lean side facing down, on top of the bed of onions. Roast pork in a preheated oven @375 degrees for about 40 minutes until onions are caramelized. Remove onions and all the dark sauce for gravy.
Continue roasting the pork loin for another 45-50 minutes. Roasting time is approximately 22 minutes per pound of meat. A meat thermometer in the roast showing an internal temperature of 180 degrees indicates the meat is done.

Heat onions in a Teflon pan with 2 cups red wine, 2 Tbsp of double deluxe soy sauce, 1 Tbsp of dark soy sauce, and 2 Tbsp of raw sugar to achieve a rich dark glaze. Season to taste. Discard star anise. Serve sliced pork loin surrounded by caramelized onions on a large serving platter. An electric slicer makes it easy to cut roast into thin slices. Garnish with four cups of cooked broccoli florets surrounding the pork and serve sauce in a separate bowl. The pork loin is lean and tender, while the onions are sensational making this an **Easy, Healthy and Delicious** entrée that serves a large number of people.

Banana Bread & Lemon Poppy Seed Bread

Breads and Soups

Breads

Banana Bread
Lemon Poppy Seed Bread / Cake
Cheese Bread
Garlic Bread

Soups

Celadon Bisque / Spinach Bisque
Shrimp & Corn Chowder
Crabmeat Bisque

Picture from top left to right.
Cake Base for **Heavenly Fruit Torte** made with Lemon Poppy Seed Bread Basket of **Banana Poppy Seed Muffins** and **Lemon Poppy Seed Muffins** Loaf of **Banana Bread**

Mini Loaf of Lemon Poppy Seed Bread that can be served as a cake or used as a cake base cut into 1/3 inch squares (without seeds,) for the **Low Calorie Trifle** or sliced for cake bases for **Strawberry Bavarian Torte** or **Ice Cream Cake**. See recipes for these desserts.

137

♥ Banana Bread

1 cup whole wheat flour
8 Tbsp unsalted butter or margarine
7/8 cup sugar
3 ripe bananas (large)

2 eggs
1tsp baking soda
1/4 cup oatmeal
Poppy seeds

Grease and flour an 8-1/2 inch loaf pan.
Mix bananas in a blender or food processor until they are finely mashed.
Cream butter, sugar and eggs in a large mixing bowl; add mashed bananas and mix. Add flour and baking soda, and mix 'til well blended. Add oatmeal. Pour into baking pan or fill 3/4 full cup cake liners in muffin pans. Top with poppy seeds.

Bake 45-55min until lightly brown @ 350 preheated oven, for loaf pans.
Bake 20-30 minutes if using muffin pans.
Banana bread is done when a wooden skewer comes out clean. Convection ovens generally bake a little faster than conventional ovens. Banana bread can be frozen and reheated in a toaster oven or served cold. It is a nutritious breakfast food or snack. The **Easy, Healthy and Delicious Banana Bread** tastes soooo good.

Lemon Poppy Seed Bread

1 package yellow cake mix
3.4-ozs package instant lemon pudding
1/2 cup oil, 1 cup water, 4 eggs
Lemon zest from one lemon (optional)
Poppy seeds (Last ingredient to be added or omitted, depending on the cake base)

Lemon Glaze
2 Tbsp butter or margarine
2 Tbsp sugar
2 Tbsp lemon juice, 1/2 cup water
1/2 tsp pure lemon extract

Mix the cake and pudding mixes; add oil, water, and eggs and mix until the batter is moist. Add lemon zest. Do not over mix. Sprinkle poppy seeds and mix with batter; pour into 3/4 full mini loaf pans and sprinkle seeds on top.

Bake in preheated oven @ 350 degrees for 25-35 minutes. Melt butter and sugar; add water, lemon juice and extract and bring to a boil. As soon as the bread comes out of the oven, loosen bread from the sides of the pan. Pour hot glaze over the bread when it is still in the pan.

This is an **Easy and Delicious** bread that has the refreshing aroma of lemon. It's a versatile recipe that can be doubled and used for the **Heavenly Fruit Torte (use a greased and floured torte pan), Low Calorie Trifle** and Strawberry Bavarian Torte and Coffee Mouse Torte. Freeze the cake bases (unglazed, with no poppy seeds in the batter) for the above desserts, and you save yourself a lot of time. **See Photo** of breads and **Photo** of Heavenly Fruit Torte with the torte bake pan in the dessert section.

Cheese Bread

1 cup grated cheddar
1 cup grated Monterey Jack
3/8 cup light mayonnaise
1 stalk scallion, diced

1/4 cup chives, diced
Johnny's Garlic Spread Seasoning, a sprinkling
1 loaf French bread (not sourdough)

Cut the French bread lengthwise in half and sprinkle lightly with garlic spread seasoning. Mix cheeses, mayonnaise, scallions, & chives in a bowl and spread on both halves of bread. Cut into 2-inch serving pieces first.

Wrap the half loaves in foil and bake in preheated oven @400 degrees for 20min. Open foil and turn oven to broil, monitoring the bread until cheese bubbles. Do not let it burn. Serve hot. Cheese bread is an **Easy, Healthy and Delicious** bread with melted cheese fresh from the oven. Serves 10.

 Garlic Bread

French bread (not sourdough)
Johnny's Garlic Spread Seasoning
Canola oil spray, olive oil spray, or light mayonnaise

Slice French bread lengthwise, then into serving sizes. For smaller quantities, slice into 1/4-inch diagonals. Bakeries can slice the bread diagonally or straight with a bread slicer.

Spread mayonnaise, or spray the sliced French bread with canola oil; thinly spread garlic spread on bread and broil on low until it's lightly crusted and golden. Leave oven door open and watch carefully that the bread does not burn.
Unused portions of sliced fresh bread without seasoning can be frozen.
All the breads are **Easy, Healthy and Delicious.**

♥ Celadon Bisque / Spinach Bisque

3 cups chicken broth
3 cups soy milk or whole milk
1 large peeled and sliced potato
1/3 cup prewashed baby spinach,

1/4 tsp garlic powder, salt and white pepper
2-5 Tbsp potato flour
Croutons, a sprig of mint

Boil potato in 1 cup chicken broth until soft enough to mash.
Mix spinach, cooked potato, and 2 1/2 cups of chicken broth in a blender (liquefy) until the texture is smooth. Heat the blender mixture with milk and bring it to a boil. Mix 2-4 Tbsp of potato flour in a small bowl with 1/2 cup of chicken broth and whisk in potato flour mixture into the hot soup over medium heat, stirring constantly until well blended. Whisk in more potato flour mixed with a little broth first and then add to the boiling soup if you like a thick creamy bisque. The soup thickens as you cook it. Season to taste. Garnish with croutons and a sprig of mint.

The Spinach Bisque is an Easy, Healthy and Delicious soup with the pale green color of celadon china. If you are serving this soup to children and want to give them more spinach, you could add 2-3 cups of spinach and get a darker shade of green. Serves 4-6.
Spinach is chock full of Vitamin A & C and rich with potassium and magnesium.

Shrimp and Corn Chowder

1/2 lb cooked bay shrimp, or shelled and deveined shrimp, diced
1 large peeled and sliced potato
1 8-oz can or 1 cup whole corn kernels, frozen or canned
2 cups whole or 2% low fat milk or soy milk (Vanilla)
2 cups chicken broth

2 Tbsp butter or margarine
2-4 Tbsp potato flour
1/4 tsp garlic powder, salt, white pepper
2 Tbsp pale dry sherry
Dash of cayenne pepper
Croutons
Fresh parsley or a sprig of mint leaf for garnish

Boil sliced potato in 1 cup chicken broth until soft enough to mash with a fork, or use a blender. Combine mixture with 1/2 cup chicken broth, milk, wine, garlic powder and bring everything to a boil on medium heat. Mix 2-4 Tbsp of potato flour with 1/2 cup of cold chicken broth in a small separate bowl. Whisk in blended potato flour mixture to the rest of the soup over medium heat until soup is boiling and well blended. Add more potato flour by first mixing with a little broth in a separate bowl and then whisking the mixture with the rest of the soup if you like thick, creamy chowder.

Add shrimp and corn (entire can of corn with liquid.) Bring to a boil again. Season to taste with salt and pepper. Garnish with a sprig of fresh parsley or mint leaf, croutons, and a dash of cayenne pepper. Serve the **Easy and Delicious** Shrimp and Corn Chowder piping hot. The hearty chowder serves 4. The recipe can easily be doubled.

Crabmeat Bisque

2 cups of crab soup* or chicken stock
2 1/2 cups whole or 2% low fat milk
1 large potato, peeled and sliced
1/2 cup crab meat
1 Tbsp crab paste, see photo of ingredients
2 Tbsp sherry or white cooking wine

1/2 cup corn kernels, fresh, frozen, or canned
2-4 Tbsp potato flour
3 cloves garlic, minced and sautéed in oil
Salt, white pepper
Croutons
Sprig of mint or parsley for garnish

*I make the crab bisque only when there is stock already made from the Crab Tsiuzhou Style. See Recipe under Seafood in the Chinese Cuisine section.

Boil potato in 1 1/2 cups chicken or crab stock for 15-20 minutes before whirling it in a blender until it's smooth.
Heat blended potato with 2 cups of milk to a boil. Sauté minced garlic with butter, then add crab paste, sherry, salt and white pepper and add to the soup. Mix potato flour with 1/2 cup of cold broth in a small bowl and whisk into the boiling broth over medium heat. If you like a thick bisque, put more potato flour mixed with a little cold broth in a separate bowl and whisk into the boiling soup until well blended. Add corn and crab meat and season to taste.

Serve Crab Bisque with croutons, and garnish with a sprig of mint or parsley. The Crab Bisque is an **Easy and Delicious** bisque if you have the soup base already made from a previous dinner. Serves 4.

Grilled Chicken Filet with Organic Green Salad

Salads, Vegetables, Drinks

♥ Baby Spinach Salad

Pre-washed baby spinach
1/2 cup dried cranberries
8-ozs mandarin orange
sections, drained
5 white mushrooms, sliced
1/2 cup toasted pine nuts or
slivered almonds
1 avocado, sliced

Dressing
3 Tbsp apple cider vinegar
3 Tbsp honey
1 Tbsp mustard
1 tsp finely chopped onions
11/2 Tbsp parsley
3/4 cup olive oil

This recipe makes a large quantity of dressing, which can be refrigerated and stored in a jar to toss another salad. An **Easy, Healthy and Delicious Salad** can be tossed in minutes. Mix cider vinegar and honey. Whisk mustard, onions, parsley, and oil. Add vinegar, honey, cranberries, and nuts to the mixture. Toss baby spinach and mushrooms with enough salad dressing to wet the salad greens and ingredients. Add mandarin oranges and avocado slices on top.

♥ Persimmon Spinach Salad

4-5 persimmons (Fuyu) peeled, cut
4 cups pre-washed baby spinach
1 cup of hearts of palm (6ozs,) drained

1/2 cup walnuts
1/2 cup raisins
1/2 cup Salad Toppins

Same Dressing as Baby Spinach Salad

Fuyu is shaped like an apple and can be peeled and eaten and used in a salad, while the cone shaped persimmon needs to be fully ripen and soft before eaten.
The Persimmon Salad is an **Easy, Healthy and Delicious** salad that has a sweet and tangy flavor of apple cider vinegar and honey, complemented with colorful persimmons and hearts of palm. Persimmons and spinach are chock full of Vitamin A & C and rich with minerals, especially potassium, copper and magnesium.

♥ Watercress and Organic Green Salad

1 bunch watercress
1 bag organic salad greens, or fresh
salad greens
1/2 cup mini cherry tomatoes
7 ozs hearts of palm, cut into 1/2-inch
pieces
1 jar (6.5 oz) marinated artichoke hearts,
hearts cut in half
1/2 cup small white mushrooms, sliced
1/2 cup walnuts
1/4 cup Salad Toppins (optional)
1/4 cup blue cheese, finely crumbled, or
mashed with a fork
1-2 Tbsp olive oil

Place salad greens on bottom of a large
serving plate; add sprigs of watercress, tomatoes, walnuts, blue cheese, artichoke hearts, and
hearts of palm mounded on top of the greens. Sprinkle marinade from the artichoke hearts on
the salad; top with McCormick Salad Toppins (optional).

The appeal of this salad is the vibrant display of color and the contrasts in taste of the fresh
watercress and salad greens with hearts of palm, artichoke hearts, and tangy blue cheese.
This is an **Easy and Delicious** salad using just the marinade from the artichoke hearts to toss
the salad. It's ready in 10 minutes. Serves 4 -6.

♥ Snow White Persimmon Salad

Ripe persimmons (cone shaped)
Low fat or non fat cottage cheese
Butter lettuce

Snow White Persimmon Salad is a weight watcher's dream lunch. The cone shaped
persimmons that are soft and fully ripe make a beautiful and delicious lunch served with
cottage cheese on a leaf of butter lettuce. Cottage cheese is ninety percent protein and
persimmons are loaded with vitamins A & C, and rich with minerals, potassium, copper,
and magnesium. This is a **Healthy, Easy and Delicious** salad.

Pomelo and Crabmeat Salad

1 large pomelo
1/2 cup crabmeat
1 avocado, sliced
1 bag pre-washed salad greens
1/2 cup raisins
2 Tbsp pine nuts
1 cup white mushrooms, sliced
6.5 oz jar marinated artichoke hearts
1-2 Tbsp olive oil

The pomelo looks like a gigantic cone-shaped grapefruit with a very thick rind. Choose a large heavy pomelo as the weight is often an indication of a sweet juicy fruit inside the thick yellow rind. Pomelo tastes like a sweet orange-grapefruit. Use a sharp knife to score the pomelo into quarters. Peel off the thick rind along the quartered score markings. The white membranes around each section peel off easily. Try to keep the sections whole.

Mix the salad greens with artichoke hearts cut in halves, mushrooms, small peeled pomelo sections, raisins, nuts, olive oil and 1/2 of the dressing from the jar of marinated artichokes. Arrange peeled whole pomelo sections on top of the salad, and top with crab meat, sliced avocado, and a light sprinkling of the remaining marinade from the jar of artichoke hearts.

The pomelo is juicy and sweet and makes a delightful salad with fresh greens and other salad ingredients. This is a delectable, **Healthy** and low calorie salad.

Shrimp Salad

1/2 lb cooked bay shrimp
1 bag salad greens
1 cup small white mushrooms
1 cup mini cherry tomatoes
6.5 oz jar marinated artichoke hearts

14 oz can hearts of palm, cut into 1/2"
1/2 cup garlic and cheese croutons
1/4 cup Parmesan cheese
1-2 Tbsp olive oil

Toss artichoke hearts (cut in halves) and the artichoke marinade with salad greens, bay shrimp, tomatoes, mushrooms, and Parmesan cheese. Add 1/2 can cut hearts of palm and season to taste. Scatter remaining 1/2 can cut hearts of palm and croutons on top of the salad. This is another **Easy and Delicious** salad.

❤ Tropical Salad

1 bag of fresh salad greens
1/2 can of hearts of palm (14 ozs)
2 Tbsp Orange Muscat Champagne Vinegar, Trader Joe's 8.5 ozs
1 cup small white mushrooms, sliced
1 cup mango cubes and/or 2 kiwis
1 avocado, sliced
1 cup mini cherry tomatoes
1/2 cup croutons
2-3 Tbsp olive oil
Salt, white pepper, 1 Tbsp sugar

Peel and cut mango into cubes. Peel and slice kiwis. Cut hearts of palm to 1/2 " pieces.
Mix Orange Muscat Champagne Vinegar with olive oil and sugar. Toss 3/4 of the dressing
with salad greens, mushrooms, and tomatoes. Top salad with sliced avocado, sliced hearts
of palm, mango, kiwis, and croutons. Pour remaining dressing on salad.   The tropical salad
is **Healthy, Easy, and Delicous.** Serves 4-6

146

♥ Grilled Chicken Filet with Organic Green Salad

1/2 chicken breast filet
Organic salad greens, 1 avocado
2 Tbsp Orange Muscat
Champagne Vinegar (Trader Joe's 8.5 oz)
3 Tbsp olive oil
1/8 tsp baking powder and 1 Tbsp water

2 cloves crushed garlic
Salt, white pepper, garlic powder
Dash of light soy sauce
Dash of oyster sauce, sugar
Fresh nectarine or peach
6 inch skewers, Canola oil spray, optional

You will love this nutritious and low calorie salad that is not only delicious and substantial but also colorful and fragrant.

Remove fat and tendon from chicken filet. Hold knife horizontally to slice chicken filet into 1/4 inch sheets. Marinate sliced chicken with baking soda and water to tenderize the meat. Season lightly with salt, white pepper, crushed garlic, garlic powder, a dash of light soy sauce and oyster sauce, and 1 tsp olive oil for 30 minutes.

Soak the bamboo skewers for 30 minutes in water before skewering the chicken filet. Broil skewered filet flat on foil lined pan for 5 minutes on high. Turn over and broil 1-2 minutes until chicken is done. Do not over broil. Spray grilled chicken with canola oil, optional. Mix 2 Tbsp Orange Muscat Champagne Vinegar with 2 1/2 Tbsp olive oil, salt, white pepper, garlic powder, and 1 Tbsp sugar and toss dressing with salad greens. Mix more dressing for more salad greens. Top salad with hot or cold grilled chicken and sliced avocados. Add fresh fruit if desired. The salad is **Healthy, Delicious, and Beautiful**. 2 generous servings.

♥ Layered Yam and Spinach

4 medium red yams, peeled, about 2 lbs
5 cups pre-washed spinach, packed tight

3 eggs, 1 tsp honey mustard
2 tsp oil, salt, white pepper, garlic powder

Beat 3 eggs. Microwave peeled yam for 5 minutes. Shred peeled yam in a food processor. Mix 2 1/2 beaten eggs with shredded yam, 2 tsp oil, salt and pepper. Set aside.
Microwave spinach for 1 minute until leaves are limp. Squeeze out excess water. Mix 1/2 beaten egg with spinach, honey mustard, garlic powder, salt and pepper in a food processor for a split second.

Line a loaf pan with a large piece of parchment paper (so that the loaf can be lifted easily after baking). Put 1/2 portion of yam mixture on the bottom of pan; evenly layer the spinach on top. Place remaining 1/2 of yam mixture on top. Smooth out each layer of yam and spinach so that the orange and green colors show clearly when baked and cut.

Preheat the oven to 400 degrees. Cover the loaf pan loosely with foil and bake in a Bain Marie (a roasting pan filled with hot water halfway up the sides of the loaf pan).
Bake 1 hr or until a wooden skewer comes out clean. Spray loaf lightly with canola oil. Serves 8-10.

Layered Yam and Spinach is chock full of vitamins A, C, Folate, Potassium, Magnesium, Calcium, and Copper. It is exceptionally nutritious and colorful.

148

♥ Fresh Roasted Vegetables

Red yam, peeled
Baby carrots
Parsnip, Leek, remove strings
Egg plant, sliced

Beets, peeled and sliced
Bell peppers: red, green, yellow, cut
Zucchini, cut
Mushrooms

Seasoning: Olive oil, salt, white pepper, garlic chopped, Herbes de Provence or Italian dressing. Add 1-2 tsp honey and a dash of balsamic vinegar later.

Peel yam and slice diagonally in thin 1/8 inch pieces. Mix olive oil and seasoning with vegetables. Roast beets 5 minutes first at 375 degrees; add yam, carrots, parsnip, leek, and egg plants and roast 10 minutes. Add bell peppers, zucchini and mushrooms. Stir when adding vegetables and roast vegetables 15 minutes more.

Add honey and a dash of balsamic vinegar and roast another 5 minutes. You can add or delete vegetables according to your preference. Roasting time varies, so check periodically and remove any that are done. The Fresh Roasted Vegetables are **Easy, Healthy, Delicious**, low calorie, and nutritiously packed with vitamins and minerals.

♥ Sangria

1 bottle of red wine, 2 quarts of Collins Mix, Sugar
Combination of any 3 or more of these fresh fruit: Navel orange, 1/2 apple, 1 banana, grapes, nectarine, peach.

Peel orange in one long swirl. Cut orange into cubes. Use a large punch bowl to mix cubed oranges, apples, and other fruit, orange peel, wine, Collins Mix, and some sugar to taste. This is a favorite wine punch that is frequently served with dinner in Spain. If you like the Sangria strong, use more wine, if you like it mild, use more Collins Mix. The Spaniards like their Sangria strong as I remember getting tipsy drinking it. At home I make mine fairly mild. Refrigerate 3 hours or more. The fruit tastes great with the wine punch. It's a wonderful punch for outdoor dining. The proportions are so flexible that you could make a large or small quantity to suit your taste and needs. The Sangria is an **Easy, Healthy and Delicious** wine punch.

♥ Smoothie

1/2 orange, 1 banana, peeled
1/2 pear or apple, cored and unpeeled

2 cups soy milk, or 2% low fat milk
1 Tbsp ground flaxseeds

Cut pear and banana into large chunks with orange sections. Put all the ingredients with one cup of soy milk into a blender. Blend first, and then liquefy for 1-2 minutes until the texture is smooth.
Add the second cup of soy milk and blend for a few seconds.
You can add strawberries, seedless grapes, mango, orange juice or other seasonal fruit.

Flaxseeds are rich in omega-3 fatty acids. Flaxseeds can be purchased at health food stores, and ground with a coffee grinder and stored in the refrigerator until ready to use in drinks and cereal. Smoothie is nutritious **Easy, Healthy and Delicious.**

Desserts

Ice Cream Cake, Apple Torte, Rum Cake with a dark moist rum glaze. Rum Cake with a golden glaze by twice inverting the cake. The rum cakes taste the same but look quite different.

♥ Heavenly Fruit Torte

The Heavenly Fruit Torte is a beautiful, low calorie dessert that delights fruit lovers. Plan ahead by baking the cake base when making the Lemon Poppy Seed Bread or Rum Cake. Then the only thing to make is the pastry cream; slice the fruit and lightly glaze it.

You can also buy a fluted cake bottom (with a round well in the middle for the custard) from the supermarket or make one from scratch. When you bake the **Lemon Poppy Seed** Bread, before the poppy seeds are added, use part of the batter for the **Heavenly Fruit Torte**.

Spray the fluted torte pan with canola oil spray and dust the greased pan with flour. Fill the pan half full with batter and bake in a preheated oven @ 350 degrees for 15-20 min until done. The torte cake base can be frozen until you are ready to use it.

Pastry Cream for the fruit torte
4 tsp flour, 3 Tbsp sugar
4 tsp cornstarch
1 egg and 1 egg yolk
1 1/4 cups low fat or soy milk (Silk, Vanilla)
1/2 tsp vanilla
1/2 tsp lemon extract, lemon or lime juice

Mix flour, sugar, and cornstarch in a small mixing bowl. Set aside.
Beat egg and egg yolk until thick. Heat milk over medium heat and whisk in egg mixture. Cook and stir with a whisk over medium heat.
In a small separate bowl, briskly whisk flour with 1/4 cup of the hot milk mixture until the texture is very smooth; then combine with the rest of the milk mixture in the pot, whisking and cooking over medium until pastry cream thickens. Add vanilla and lemon extracts and whisk. Cool.

Fresh Fruit Topping
Choose any fruit: peaches, white peaches, white nectarines (with peel), pears, blueberries, kiwi, strawberries 1 Tbsp strained apricot jam (use a spoon to put jam through a fine sieve.)

Dip peeled and sliced fresh pear in a little lemon or lime juice and sugar so that it does not turn brown. Strawberries and blueberries don't need dipping; they add color contrast.

Turn the cake base over and fill the well with pastry cream.
Decorate the torte with abundant sliced fruit, placed in concentric circles on top of pastry cream. Use a pastry brush to lightly coat the fruit with strained apricot to give it a shiny glaze. Sprinkle blueberries on top for color accent.

The Heavenly Fruit Torte is a dazzling healthy and low calorie winner. **See Photo of Heavenly Fruit Torte and torte pan.**

Bavarian Mousse

3 envelopes unflavored gelatin
3 3/4 cups milk
5 egg yolks, 6 egg whites, separated
1 1/4 cup sugar
1/4 cup dark rum
1 cup heavy cream, whipped
3/4 cup crushed almond macaroons (very light and crispy) or Vanilla wafers
1/2 cup chopped walnuts
Canola oil spray
Teflon coated Bundt cake pan

Whip cream until peaks form, then refrigerate.
Sprinkle gelatin into 1 cup milk. Let gelatin soften. Heat 2 3/4 cups milk in the top of a double boiler over direct heat until tiny bubbles appear around edge.

In a medium bowl, beat egg yolks with 1/2 cup sugar until well blended. Add softened gelatin. Whisk egg and gelatin mixture into hot milk and continue simmering on top of double boiler for 8-10 minutes until gelatin is dissolved. Stir with a whisk and add rum.

Remove from double boiler. To hasten chilling, put the bowl with the gelatin mixture on a bed of ice for about 30-40 minutes. Stir occasionally with whisk while chilling.

Beat egg whites in a large bowl until they form soft peaks. Gradually add 3/4 cup sugar until stiff peaks form. Add whippped cream and chilled gelatin mixture. Beat at low speed for 1 minute until mixture is blended.

Spray the Bundt pan with canola oil spray. In a food processor, mix macaroons and nuts for 1 minute until finely crumbled. Blend 1/3 of the nuts and macaroons into the whipped cream and gelatin mixture; pour mousse into a Teflon bundt pan. Refrigerate 5 hours.
Invert the Bundt pan onto a serving plate and top the mousse with the remainder of nuts and macaroon crumbs.

The Bavarian Mousse can also be elegantly served in small wine glasses.
The Bavarian Mousse will appeal to a gourmet's palate. It is light, creamy, and delectable, truly a little slice of heaven. This recipe serves 12 or more.

Coffee Mousse Torte

1 mini loaf of glazed rum cake
3 envelopes unflavored gelatin
3 3/4 cups milk
5 yolks, 6 egg whites, separated
1 cup sugar
1/4 cup coffee liqueur
1 tsp granulated instant coffee
1 cup heavy cream, whipped
3/4 cup crushed almond macaroons or
vanilla wafers
1/2 cup chopped walnuts
Canola oil spray
13"x 9 "x 2" Pyrex dish or bake pan

The Coffee Mousse Torte is a variation of the Bavarian Mousse. It's a **gourmet dessert** that is light and delectable. I make the Coffee Mousse Torte only when I have a mini loaf of rum cake already made (by doubling the ingredients when the rum cake was made and the extra loaves frozen.) If you don't have the rum cake ready, then make the Coffee Mousse in a smaller quantity and serve it like a parfait in elegant wine glasses without the rum cake base.

Cut rum cake (a mini loaf) into 1/4 inch thin slices and line a 13"x 9 "x 2" Pyrex dish or baking pan to create the base for the torte. Set aside.

Whip cream until peaks form, then refrigerate. Sprinkle gelatin into 1 cup milk to soften gelatin about 10 minutes.

Heat 2 3/4 cups milk in the top of a double boiler over direct heat until tiny bubbles appear around edge.

In a medium bowl, beat egg yolks with 1/2 cup sugar until well blended. Add softened gelatin. Slowly whisk mixture into hot milk and simmer on top of double boiler. Add coffee liqueur.

Remove bowl from double boiler. To hasten chilling, put the bowl with the gelatin mixture on a bed of ice surrounding the bowl for about 30 minutes. Stir occasionally with whisk.

Beat egg whites in a large bowl until they form soft peaks. Gradually add 1/4 cup sugar until stiff peaks form. Add whippped cream and chilled gelatin mixture. Beat at low speed for 1 minute until mixture is blended.

In a food processor or blender, mix macaroons and nuts for 1 minute until finely crumbled. Blend 1/3 of the nuts and macaroons into the whipped cream and gelatin mixture; pour mousse on top of the thinly sliced rum cake base. Sprinkle remainder of cookie mix on top of the mousse. Refrigerate 5 hours or overnight.

The Coffee Mousse Torte is an epicurean delight and is one of my favorite creations. Coffee connoisseurs will enjoy the aroma and taste of the luscious liqueur. Serves 12-15.

♥ Apple Torte

7/8 cup sugar
4 oz. unsalted butter, or margarine
2 eggs
1 cup whole wheat flour

1 tsp baking powder
1-2 apples, unpeeled, cored, cut into
quarters, then twelfths
Sugar & cinnamon

Mix sugar and butter. Add eggs and mix until batter is smooth. Mix flour and baking powder in a separate bowl and add to batter. Mix on medium and pour batter into ungreased baking pans. Put sliced apples in two concentric circles on top of the batter. Sprinkle lightly with cinnamon and sugar.
Bake in preheated oven @ 350 for 35-55 minutes, depending on the oven and the size of the baking pan. Bake until lightly crusted. You can use a 9 inch spring form pan for a large torte, or small pie plates for smaller tortes.

Serve warm or cold with ice cream. Serves 6-10 depending on size of torte.

The apple torte can also be made with 1/2 whole wheat and 1/2 white flour, giving the torte a lighter color and texture when baked, while the all whole wheat flour has the healthy whole grain appeal.

The apple torte looks so tantalizing with a light crust and glazed apples decorating the torte. Your family and friends will think you got it from a fancy bakery! Apples can be substituted with other fruit. Pears or peaches are great too, as long as the fruit is not too juicy. **The Apple Torte** is an **Easy, Healthy and Delicious dessert** that can be whipped up in a jiffy. It is such a family favorite that I often double or quadruple the recipe as the torte can be frozen and reheated easily.

Butter Rum Cake

1 package yellow cake mix
1 package instant vanilla pudding (3.4 ozs)
1/2 cup oil
1 cup water
4 eggs
1/2 cup chopped walnuts (optional)

Rum Glaze
7 ozs butter or margarine
1/4 cup sugar
1/2 cup rum
1/2 cup water

Grease and flour a bundt cake pan. Scatter chopped nuts on bottom of pan. (optional)
Mix the cake ingredients until the batter is moist. Do not over mix.
Bake in preheated oven @ 350 degrees 40-55 minutes, or until a thin wooden skewer comes out clean.
While the cake is being baked, melt butter and sugar in a pan. Add water and bring it to a boil; add rum and bring it to a boil again.

As soon as the cake comes out of the oven, use a wooden skewer to loosen the sides and center of the cake so that it will come out easily from the bundt pan. Immediately pour bubbling rum glaze over the cake when it is hot and still in the pan. The glaze easily soaks into the cake when it is hot. Use a long bamboo skewer to help the glaze seep into the sides and center of the cake. After pouring 3/4 of the glaze on the cake, invert the cake onto a serving plate and pour the rest of the glaze over the cake.

The photo on the left shows the rum cake with a dark moist glaze when you invert it. You have the option of inverting the cake a second time if you want the rum cake to have a **golden** glaze as in the photo on the right.
The two rum cakes taste the same but look totally different.

By doubling the ingredients of the Butter Rum Cake, you can have a rum cake and the base for several other desserts (**Low Calorie Trifle, the Heavenly Fruit Torte, Ice Cream Cake, Coffee Mousse Torte, and Strawberry Bavarian Torte).** Bake the second batch of the batter in a torte cake pan and a couple of mini loaf pans. Freeze the cake bases (unglazed) for the other desserts and save yourself a lot of time. The base for the Coffee Mousse Torte should be glazed.

This is an **Easy and Delicious** cake that has an enticing fragrance of rum.
Friends will remember you for making such a mouth-watering **gourmet dessert.**

Ice Cream Cake

1 small package of chocolate Oreos or a few slices of rum or lemon cake
1 box of rolled cookies, cut into 3 inch half lengths (optional ingredient)
Half gallon of your favorite ice cream
1 1/2 Tbsp vegetable oil

Leave ice cream at room temperature for about 15 minutes.
Crumble 15 Oreo cookies in the Cuisinart until it's finely crumbled. Mix cookie crumbs with oil and line the bottom of a spring form pan. Press and smooth out the cookie mix.
If you have a mini loaf of lemon or rum cake (See recipes) ready in the freezer, then slice the cake into 1/4 inch pieces to fill the bottom of a spring form pan in place of the cookie crumbs.
Cut and line the rolled cookies around the sides of the spring form pan.
Spread ice cream on top of the cookie mix or the sliced cake. Smooth out the ice cream.
Cover the spring form pan with foil and freeze. Defrost the ice cream cake for 5-10 minutes and transfer to serving plate. **See Photo of Ice Cream Cake.**

This is my sister, Lily's favorite dessert for the kids' parties. Adults love it too. I added the rolled cookies for a more festive touch, but the ice cream cake is delicious without the rolled cookies and good with either crumbled Oreos or sliced lemon or rum cake base.

Biscotti di Prato

4 oz. unsalted butter, or margarine
2 cups whole wheat flour, 1 1/2 cup flour
1 1/4 cup sugar
1 Tbsp baking powder
3 eggs
1t vanilla
1t almond
1 cup chopped almonds

Mix flour, sugar, and baking powder; add butter.
Whisk eggs, vanilla and almond flavors. Add to batter and mix; add almonds last.
Make 4 rectangular logs that are slightly flattened on top.

Bake in preheated oven @ 350 for 30 minutes. Take out from oven and cool 20-30 minutes.
Cut into 1/2 inch diagonals. Turn over and bake another 10 min on each side, until all four sides are baked and crispy. After the last 10 minutes, turn off the oven and leave the batch overnight without opening the oven door.
Store in jars.
This biscotti is very crispy and can be addictive for people who like crunchy foods. Dip in coffee or tea, as the Italians do.

Best Chocolate Chip Cookies

3/4 cup butter
2/3 cup sugar, 1/2 cup brown sugar
2 eggs
1/2 tsp vanilla
1 tsp baking soda

1/4 cup rolled oats
3/4 cup whole wheat flour, 3/4 cup flour
12 ozs semisweet chocolate chips
1 1/2 cup toasted macadamia nuts or walnuts

Toast macadamia nuts or walnuts in a 230 degree preheated oven for 25 minutes. Turn off oven and leave overnight without opening the oven door. (Toasting is optional).

Use a large mixing bowl to beat butter and sugars on high until fluffy. Add eggs, vanilla, and lemon juice and mix well.
In a separate bowl, mix flour, baking soda, and rolled oats. Add to creamed mixture in the large bowl and blend well. Add chocolate chips and nuts.

Grease cookie sheet. Spoon 1/4 cup cookie dough onto cookie sheet, 3 inches apart. Flatten cookie dough slightly. Bake in preheated 350 degrees oven for 14-16 minutes.
Cool cookies on rack. This recipe makes 18 oversized cookies.
These are the best homemade chocolate chip cookies, really **Easy and Delicious.**

Decadent Brownies

6 Tbsp butter or margarine
1 cup + 1/2 cup chocolate bits
2 eggs
1/2 cup sugar

1/4 cup flour, 1/4 cup whole wheat flour
1/2 tsp. baking powder
1/2 tsp. vanilla
3/4 cup chopped nuts

Melt butter and 1 cup chocolate bits on low. Watch carefully that you do not burn the chocolate. Beat eggs and sugar; add flour and baking powder. Mix and add melted chocolate, vanilla, and chopped nuts. Just before baking, toss 1/2 cup of chocolate bits into the batter and stir to wet the chocolate bits.

Bake in 8 inch greased pan in a 375 degree preheated oven for 25 minutes or until it lightly crusts on top, but the middle is still slightly wobbly. Brownies will solidify when cooled. Refrigerate.
Alternatively, to ease cutting the brownies in clean cuts, line an ungreased baking pan with parchment or aluminum paper so that the brownies can be lifted easily from the pan after baking and cooling. Cut with a sharp knife after refrigerating. It's an irresistibly **Easy and Delicious** dessert.

Scotch Shortbread

2 1/2 cups flour
1/2 cup sugar
1 cup unsalted butter, or margarine

Cream butter and sugar. Gradually add flour. Refrigerate mixed batter for a few hours.
After refrigerating the batter, mix again until it has a saudy texture. Pour into round baking pans.
Smooth out the batter with a large spoon until the top is smooth.
Bake in preheated oven @300 degrees for 30-40 minutes. Cut immediately into quarters and
then eighths while the shortbread is still in the pan. Put a serving plate over the pan and turn it
upside down to get the shortbread out in perfect form.

Scotch Shortbread goes beautifully with vanilla ice cream. This recipe makes two round pans
or 16 triangular pieces of shortbread. It's an **Easy and Delicious** cookie for afternoon tea.

Cinnamon Bundt Cake

1 package yellow cake mix
1 small package (3.4 oz) instant vanilla pudding
1/2 cup soft butter or margarine
1 tsp vanilla
4 eggs
1 cup water
1/4 cup sugar and 1 Tbsp cinnamon, mixed together
1/2 cup chopped walnuts (add to the cinnamon and sugar mixture.)

Grease and flour a Teflon Bundt baking pan.
Mix the first two dry ingredients. Add butter, vanilla, eggs, and water. Mix just enough to wet
all the batter without lumps. Do not overmix.
Pour one-third of batter into the Bundt pan, then one layer of cinnamon and sugar; repeat a
second and third time in the same order. Swirl through once with a knife.

Bake in a 350 degree preheated oven for 35-45 minutes. This is an **Easy and Delicious** winner.

Strawberry Cheese Cake

Crust
1 1/4 cup graham crackers, finely crumbled in a food processor
3 Tbsp sugar
1/4 cup unsalted butter or margarine
Cream Cheese Filling
24 oz. cream cheese
4 eggs
1 cup sugar
1 tsp vanilla
Topping
1 cup sour cream with 1/4 cup sugar
15 –18 extra large whole strawberries (for decoration)

Mix the graham cracker crumbs, sugar and melted butter and spread evenly onto a 9-inch spring form pan. Press and smooth out the crumbs with a large soup spoon.

Mix the cream cheese, eggs, and sugar in the food processor until the mixture is entirely smooth. (About 8-10 minutes.) Pour the cream cheese mixture into a mixing bowl and use a hand mixer to beat the creamy mixture for 10 minutes until it's very light and fluffy.

Pour into the graham cracker lined pan and bake in preheated oven @325 for 40minutes. Take out cheesecake and let it cool completely.

Beat 1 cup sour cream and add 1/4 cup sugar or less, adding just enough sugar to be slightly sweet. Beat until fluffy for 5 minutes. Spread on top of cooled cheesecake and bake in preheated oven @400 degrees for 5 minutes. Cool and refrigerate overnight.
Serve cold. Cheese cake can be made ahead of time and frozen in the pan.

You can make the cheesecake really festive by garnishing with whole strawberries surrounding the cheesecake, just before serving. The white cheese cake contrasts so beautifully against the red strawberries dressed in green leaves.

This is a scrumptuously light and delectable cheese cake that serves 12 or more.
The Strawberry Cheesecake is a surprisingly Easy and Delicious dessert that is an epicurean delight.

♥ Cottage Cheesecake

This is guilt-free cheesecake. It's made with fat free cottage cheese so you can enjoy it without feeling you have overindulged on a delicious dessert.

Crust
4 pieces graham crackers (5"x 2 1/2)
1 Tbsp sugar
2 Tbsp unsalted butter or margarine

Cheese Filling
32 oz. fat free cottage cheese
4 eggs, 1 cup sugar
1 tsp vanilla, 2 Tbsp flour

Place cottage cheese in a sieve on top of a dish to drain extra liquid for at least 48 hrs in a refrigerator. Mix graham cracker in a food processor until finely crumbled. Mix crumbs with sugar and melted butter and spread evenly onto a 9-inch spring form pan. Press and smooth out the crumbs with a large soup spoon. **You can half the proportions** for the crust and filling and bake the cheesecake in a small 5-inch spring form pan.

Use a blender to purée the cottage cheese, 3 egg yolks and 1 whole egg, until the mixture is silky smooth. Use a rubber scraper to mix and blend in the cheese on the sides of the blender; add 3/4 cup sugar, vanilla, and continue blending for 6-8 minutes.

Whip 3 egg whites until frothy; add 1/4 cup sugar and beat until egg whites form stiff peaks. In a deep bowl, beat cottage cheese mixture before blending in the beaten egg whites. Use a sieve to tap 2 Tbsp flour into the cottage cheese mixture and blend well. Pour mixture on top of the graham cracker lined pan and bake in a preheated oven @ 325 for 25-35 minutes. The cheesecake will jiggle a little and settle in a few hours. Cool and refrigerate overnight.
Top with fresh blueberries for color (optional.) I like it plain.

Cottage Cheesecake is a low calorie **Easy, Healthy and Delicious** dessert that will delight diet-conscious cheesecake lovers. It is a great substitute for the real McCoy, only minus the fat and cholesterol. Enjoy!

Nancy's Strawberry Bavarian Torte

2 envelopes plain gelatin
1/2 cup cold water
2/3 cup boiling water
1 1/4 cup sugar
2 cups strawberry pulp and juice
1 tsp fresh lemon juice

2 egg whites
1 cup heavy cream, whipped
2 packages of lady fingers or
1 package of lady fingers and sliced rum
or lemon cake, if already made

Soak gelatin in water for 5 min. Add boiling water and stir until dissolved. Clean and slice strawberries, or use frozen berries that are thawed. Use a potato masher to mash berries. You want to maintain some texture so a potato masher is preferable to a food processor. Add 1 cup sugar to strawberries and gelatin; chill until mixture thickens.

Beat egg whites with 1/4 cup sugar. Whip cream. Fold egg whites, then whipped cream into strawberry mixture. Line a 9 "spring form pan with lady fingers around the sides and bottom. Alternatively, bottom could be lined with 1/4 inch thin slices of butter rum cake or lemon cake if already made. See Recipes.
Pour strawberry mixture into pan and garnish top with sliced strawberries. Refrigerate at least 6 hrs. Brush sliced strawberries with 1 tsp strained apricot jam to give it a shiny glaze (optional).

This is a beautiful, healthy, and delicious dessert that will please the most discriminating gourmet. Serves 8-10.

♥ Persimmon Sorbet

When the cone-shaped persimmons are fully ripe and soft, scoop out the center into 8 oz yogurt containers and freeze. Leave frozen persimmon at room temperature for 40 minutes and enjoy an **Easy, Healthy, and Delicious** Persimmon Sorbet.

The best time to make the persimmon sorbet is when you have an overly abundant supply of fresh ripe persimmons that need to be consumed right away. Persimmons have lots of Vitamin A (an average Fuyu has more than 3000 I.U.) & C and are high in potassium and magnesium.

♥ Fresh Mango Pudding

3 cups of mango purée (2 large, ripe mangos)
3 envelopes unflavored gelatin
3/4 cup sugar

1 1/2 cups mango juice
1 cup 2 % (low fat) evaporated milk

Mangos will ripen faster if placed in an enclosed brown bag with a few apples.
Refrigerate 1/2 cup mango juice until it's quite cold.
Cut fresh mango into 2 large slices and scoop out the fruit using a large serving spoon. Use the spoon to scoop out the remaining fruit around the core.   Purée mango in a blender for 1 1/2-2 minutes until the texture is silky smooth.

Soften gelatin in 1 cup mango juice for 5 minutes. Heat juice on medium; add sugar and stir until gelatin and sugar are completely dissolved. Add refrigerated mango juice and mix until blended. Keep mixing and don't let the juice and gelatin jell.
Whisk mango purée with evaporated milk. Combine mango juice mixture with the mango purée and whisk until the mixture is very smooth. Pour into individual serving dishes or a 6 1/2 -inch oiled Teflon mold and refrigerate 4 hrs. Garnish pudding with a sprig of mint leaf. The Fresh Mango Pudding is a healthy, deliciously light, nutritious, and low calorie treat that you could indulge yourself again and again. Mangos are rich in Vitamin A, Potassium, and Copper.
Serves 6-8.

Fruit Cake

6 ozs unsalted butter or margarine
1 1/3 cup sugar
6 egg whites, 5 egg yolks
1 12-oz pkg vanilla wafers

2 cups walnuts, slightly crumbled (30 seconds in the food processor)
1 cup coconut flakes, 2 cups raisins
1 dozen walnut halves

Put vanilla wafers in food processor and mix until finely crumbled.
Grease and flour a tube pan very carefully as the cake tends to stick to the bottom of the pan.
Cream butter, sugar and eggs. Add dry ingredients and mix.
Pour batter into the tube pan and bake in preheated oven @ 325 degrees for 1 1/2 hours or until wooden skewer comes out clean.
Moisten the walnut halves and coat with sugar. Decorate the fruit cake with the walnut halves. This fruit cake has only vanilla wafers, eggs, nuts, raisins and coconut flakes. Commercial fruit cakes are often too sweet, whereas my recipe uses very little sugar and no candied dried fruit. The Fruit Cake is an **Easy and Delicious** dessert for the holidays.

❤ Frozen Banana Nuggets

Ripe bananas
Chopped walnuts
Chopped vanilla wafers

Ripe bananas make a delicious frozen dessert. Wait until the banana peels are spotted before making this dessert. Use a food processor to chop walnuts and vanilla wafers in equal proportions into fine crumbs. Cut peeled bananas into 3/4 inch pieces and coat with chopped walnuts and vanilla wafer crumbs. Place nut-coated bananas on a serving plate covered with a plastic bag and freeze. The frozen banana nuggets are **Easy, Healthy and Delicious.** It tastes like an ice cream dessert. Try it. You'll love it. Serve it straight from the freezer. My health conscious daughter gave me this idea.

 Frozen Stuffed Dates

Stuff pitted dates with walnut halves. Store in plastic sealed bag and freeze. Serve stuffed dates frozen. They are delicious and belong to the **Easy, Healthy and Delicious** Recipes.

Carrot Cake

3 cups grated carrots
2 cups whole wheat flour
2 cups brown sugar
2 tsp cinnamon
1 tsp soda
1 1/2 cups vegetable oil

4 eggs
1 cup raisins
1 1/2 cups walnuts
Frosting: 8 oz pkg cream cheese, powdered sugar, 1 tsp vanilla

Grease and flour 9x13 inch Pyrex pan.
Grate carrots in food processor.
Mix dry ingredients: flour, sugar, soda, and cinnamon. Add oil and mix until blended. Add eggs and mix. Add carrots, raisins, and nuts last.
Bake in a 325 degree preheated oven for 45 minutes. Cool and frost.

Frosting: Mix 8 oz package of cream cheese with 4-5 ozs powdered sugar and 1 tsp vanilla. Gradually add sugar until it is barely sweet; carrot cake can be served without the frosting making it an **Easy, Healthy and Delicious** cake.

Prune Cake

1/4 cup sugar
1 cup whole wheat flour
1 cup flour
2 tsp baking soda
1/4 tsp baking powder
1 1/2 tsp cinnamon
1 tsp nutmeg

1 tsp allspice
1 1/4 cup vegetable oil
3 large eggs
1 cup buttermilk
1 tsp vanilla
1 cup pitted prunes, chopped
1 cup pecans or walnuts

In a large bowl, mix dry ingredients in the left column. Set aside.
Cook prunes in boiling water for 6 minutes. Drain.
Mix oil, eggs, milk, and vanilla. Add to dry ingredients and mix. Add prunes and nuts.
Bake in greased and floured tube pan @ 350 degrees for 60 minutes.

This is an **Easy, Healthy and Delicious** cake that is quite moist.

❤ Low Calorie Trifle

The Low Calorie Trifle is created to please the calorie watchers and is served in dainty wine glasses.

Sponge cake, pound cake, or lemon cake
Choose any 3-5 assortments of fresh diced fruit: peach, nectarine, fuyu persimmon, whole grapes or blueberries. Apples, pears, and bananas have to be dipped in lemon or lime juice first so that they don't turn brown.
1/4 package almond macaroons, or 1/2 cup vanilla wafers. crumbled

Custard sauce

1 egg and one egg yolk	2 tsp tapioca starch
1/4 cup sugar	1 tsp rum extract
2 cups whole or 2% low fat milk	

Scald milk on medium heat. Beat eggs with sugar and whisk into hot milk and cook while stirring over medium heat. Add vanilla. Mix tapioca starch with 2 Tbsp milk and whisk into hot milk to thicken custard. Whisk and cook on medium for 1 minute.

Line the wineglasses with a layer of diced rum cake or lemon cake.
Add a layer of custard to wet and cover the cake.
Add a layer of mixed diced fresh fruit.
Add a layer of custard.
Add a tsp of almond macaroon crumbs.
Repeat layers ending with macaroon crumbs or fruit on top.

With advanced planning, this is an **Easy, Healthy and Delicious** dessert if you have already put aside part of the rum cake or made a mini loaf when you made the Rum Cake or Lemon Poppy Seed Bread (without the poppy seeds) by doubling the recipe.

♥ Fresh Fruit Salad

Fresh fruit salad is always a delight after any meal. Make it when fresh fruit is abundant. Serve it in a large crystal bowl or individual bowls or wineglasses. If you have a picnic, you could carve a seedless watermelon into an oval basket with a handle and scoop mini balls from the center or cut the melon into 1/2 inch cubes mixed with other fruit of your choice. We had an elaborate luncheon shower where we filled papaya halves with choice fruit. You can make it as simple or as fancy as you want.

Here are some basic and fancy fruit salad choices:

Apples, Pears, Bananas need to be cubed and quickly dipped with lemon or lime juice so that they do not turn brown.
Red and Green Seedless Grapes, Navel oranges, Cantaloupes, Honeydew adds great color and juice.
Peaches and Nectarines are popular summer time favorites.
Mangos and Papayas add great flavor.
Blueberries, Raspberries, Kiwis, and Strawberries add a very fine touch but should be added last when everything else is cut and mixed.

Choose whatever fruit is most available and appealing to you. The Fresh Fruit Salad is a refreshingly healthy **Easy, Healthy and Delicious** dessert to serve at the end of dinner.

♥ Chocolate Dipped Strawberries

1 basket of large whole strawberries
1 package of semi-sweet chocolate chips 12 ozs (premium chocolate bits)
1 sheet of wax paper

It is ideal if you can get the giant strawberries with the stems. Otherwise get the largest strawberries available.
Wash and thoroughly dry strawberries with stems and leaves intact. Melt chocolate chips in a double boiler over boiling water. You can also melt chocolate chips directly in a pan on low temperature so that the chocolate does not burn. It's easier to dip the strawberries in a pan with a generous amount of chocolate.
Hold strawberries by the stem or stem leaves and dip a little more than half of the strawberry into the melted chocolate.
Lift and put dipped strawberries on wax paper to dry. Leave at room temperature away from the sun. Serve Chocolate Dipped Strawberries on a beautiful platter.

Chocolate Dipped Strawberries are **Easy, Healthy and Delicious** after dinner desserts. They have a gorgeous catered appeal.

Index